Walks

in

MORBIHAN

Southern Brittany

36 circular walks with maps and directions, suggestions of other walks nearby and places of interest to visit

G. H. RANDALL

Walks in Morbihan, Southern Brittany
published by Red Dog Books
ISBN 978 0 9536001 8 2

© Red Dog Books 2007

British Library Cataloguing-in-Publication Data
A catalogue record for this book is available from the British Library

Red Dog Books is based in Axbridge, Somerset and in Brittany.
Enquiries should be addressed to the editorial office at
Red Dog Books, 29410 Plounéour-Ménez, France.

email: reddogbooks@tiscali.fr

www.reddogbooks.com

Printed and bound in China

ABOUT THIS BOOK

THE WALKS are arranged in order of their length, Walk No.1 being the shortest at 4kms and the last four in the book, Walk Nos.33 to 36, being about 15kms each. They are grouped and colour-coded into Short (up to 7kms - yellow), Medium (7-10kms - red) and Long walks (11kms upwards - blue).

The approximate location of each walk and its colour code for length is marked on the department map on the inside front cover. Thus it should be possible to choose a walk of the required length within reach of anywhere in the department. The walks are named according to their starting point. Some are town walks, some are coastal, some include many points of interest such as megaliths or chapels, whilst others rely on the peace of the countryside for their appeal. Each has a brief introduction to give a clue to what's in store.

In describing the walks, French terminology is used to indicate some features that do not have an adequate English name. For example, there is a traditionally Breton type of track referred to as a 'chemin creux' - literally a 'dug out road'. It is usually bordered by trees and is sunk to below the level of the surrounding land, sometimes with raised banks on either side. Where used, all such terms will be in italics and explained in the glossary on page 11.

Roads are shown on the maps in yellow. This indicates a tarmac road. For simplicity, these are usually shown at a uniform width but of course on the ground they can vary enormously. The more important roads will be 'departmental' roads and will have a 'D' number. Where these roads feature in the walk directions they will be indicated just by their number, e.g. D181. Tracks are marked on the maps by double lines in black, pathways by a single black line. Those to be followed are indicated by a series of broad arrows, alongside the tracks or overlaying the paths.

All distances given are approximate - they are there to give an indication of when to be looking for the next turning or the next point of interest.

Historical, archaeological or topographical background

information is given in brown text to distinguish it from the directions, which are in bold black so as to be more easily followed whilst walking. Diversions or alternative routes are shown in blue, both in the text and on the maps.

Illustrations for each walk have been selected to give a flavour of the scenerey to be encountered, rather than to present an image of constant sunshine.

At the end of each walk are indications of other walks that can be followed in the same area, and/or places of interest within easy reach that offer an alternative to walking. The places of interest are listed again at the end of the book, cross-referenced to their nearest walk(s). Please note that both the places of interest and the other walks are suggestions only and local Tourist Offices or mairies may have additional information.

KEY

MAP SYMBOLS

✧	archaeological or historical feature	☆	fort
✳	belvedere/viewpoint	≙	fontaine/spring
＝	bridge	◊	menhir
▬	building(s)	⊓	dolmen
Å	campsite	P	parking for start of walk
✛	château	▲	peak
♦	church	①	reference point in the directions
+	chapel		
†	calvary or wayside cross	⬭	marsh

ABBREVIATIONS
TO = tourist office
GR = long distance footpath

GRADING OF WALKS (for guidance only)
Level 1 : fairly level route
Level 2 : fairly level route with gradual climbs
Level 3 : generally up and down, paths needing care
Level 4 : one or more very steep slope and/or many steps

CONTENTS

ACKNOWLEDGEMENTS

I would first like to thank Wendy Mewes – in general for her advice and expertise, and in particular for the contribution of the two historic walks at Auray and Ploërmel. I have also found her book *Discovering the History of Brittany* invaluable background reading.

Also I would like to thank the many tourist officials and administrators whose advice has been of help in preparing this book. Deserving of special mention are staff at the *Pays d'Accueil Touristique de la Vallée du Blavet* and the *Maison du Scorff*.

A word of thanks too for the many unseen, anonymous people who regularly and assiduously maintain footpaths and tracks so that others may enjoy them.

WALKING IN MORBIHAN

Brittany offers an excellent environment for walkers: the climate is temperate, the countryside is beautiful and largely unspoilt, the forests are deep, the rivers are characterful, the coast is alternately spectacular and gentle. Furthermore, there is always something particular to see, some dolmen, some fontaine, some chapel, some site of legend, some relic of history to give a purpose to your walk and a memory to cherish.

Morbihan is the department that sits in the middle of southern Brittany. Its name, *mor bihan*, is Breton for 'little sea', a reference to the Gulf of Morbihan where hundreds of tiny islands are scattered across an area of calm water, connected to but sheltered from the Atlantic ocean. The department is best known for its neolithic remains, the most famous of which are the alignments of menhirs at Carnac. Other sites, range from the excavated, reconstructed and carefully managed Dolmen of the Merchant's Table and Great Broken Menhir at Locmariaquer to the remote and mystical menhirs that can be encountered quite unexpectedly in the landscape.

Water is a recurring feature of walking in Morbihan. Apart from the Gulf of Morbihan and the southern coast, there is the *Lac au Duc* just north of Ploërmel, the largest natural lake in Brittany, the artificial *Lac de Guerlédan* on the northern border with Côtes d'Armor, and the Nantes-Brest Canal weaving its way across the north eastern part of the department. The major rivers, the *Blavet*, the *Oust*, and the *Scorff* provide tranquil scenery with that special quality imparted by flowing water, and many other rivers and streams, lakes and ponds are encountered along the way.

Walking is a very popular pastime in Brittany and there are endless numbers of ancient communal footpaths and tracks that can be followed. Not all of them, however, lead anywhere, which is why a guidebook is always useful. While some paths have fallen into disuse, many new ones have been recently opened up. Most footpaths are regularly maintained and kept open. Some routes do cross private land, however, and it is obviously a good idea to respect the owners' rights and privacy in order that these routes remain open for future walkers.

The countryside code is much the same in Brittany as elsewhere. Here is a typical version of it:

Porte de bonnes chaussures, et des vêtements peu fragiles.
Connais, aime et respecte la nature et le monde rural.
Écoute la nature, pas de cris ni de transistors.
Ne souille pas la nature: ce n'est pas une poubelle; remporte tes déchets.
Ne casse pas les branches, respecte les jeunes plantes.
Admire les fleurs, et plantes sauvages; ne les cueille pas.
Observe les animaux, mais ne les dérange pas.
N'effraie pas les troupeaux, referme les portes des clôtures.
Attention au feu, à la cigarette ou à l'allumette mal éteinte.
Reste sur le sentier; ne piétine ni sous-bois, ni cultures.
Attention aux vipères : munie-toi d'un bâton.
Ne néglige pas les contacts humains, engage la conversation.

Roughly translated, that is:

Wear good shoes and sturdy clothes.
Know, love and respect nature and the countryside.
Listen to nature, not to shouts and transistor radios.
Don't spoil nature - it's not a dust-bin - take your rubbish home with you.
Don't break branches - respect young plants.
Admire the flowers and wild plants - don't pick them.
Observe animals but don't disturb them.
Don't frighten herds, close gates after you.
Beware of fire, extinguish cigarettes and matches properly.
Stay on the path, don't trample the undergrowth or crops.
Beware of adders: arm yourself with a stick.
Don't ignore people you meet, engage them in conversation.

One might add keep an eye on the weather, which can be changeable, so it's advisable always to take a waterproof. A hat for protection against the sun is a good idea in summer as often there is little shade. Water to drink is essential.

WHERE ARE WE?

French *départements*, being rather large, tend to be divided into what in England would be called districts but in France are called '*pays*', as if they were independent countries. In spirit they often are, since they originate from before the revolution and are therefore older than the departments. In Brittany, until less than a hundred years ago one could tell a person's '*pays*' by the way they dressed and this 'separateness' lingers on among the older Bretons, who even today might regard themselves as natives not so much of their *département* as of their *pays*.

Officially, there are seven *pays* either completely or partially within Morbihan: *Pays de Lorient, Pays d'Auray, Pays de Vannes, Pays de Redon* (part), *Pays de Ploërmel, Pays de Pontivy,* and *Centre Ouest Bretagne* (part). However, a visitor is likely to encounter many other interpretations of how the department is divided and the parts named. Thus one is more likely to find the part of *Centre Ouest Bretagne* that lies within Morbihan referred to as the '*Pays du Roi Morvan*' (a reference to a 9th century Breton leader whose 'last stand' is thought to have been at Menez Morvan, a hill near Langonnet which is passed on Walk No.20). The naming of his stamping ground as the *Pays du Roi Morvan*, and the setting of its boundaries, is an invention of the modern tourist industry. Other names still in use today, such as *Cornouaille* and *Porhoët,* go back more legitimately to feudal times and of course their boundaries bear no relation to any post-revolutionary ones. What often happens is that individual

10

maires group their *communes* together for various economic or politcal reasons, including tourism, and then chose a name, often from history, that covers their particular area. The results can be very confusing.

MAPS
It is not intended that you should need any other map than the one printed in each walk. If you are a fan of maps, however, the best you can buy are the IGN (*Institut Géographic National*) *Série Bleue* at scale 1:25,000. These are roughly the equivalent of the Ordnance Survey pathfinders, though not quite so detailed. Some of the mapping may be quite old so be prepared to follow what's on the ground rather than the map.

GPS? well, if you must - personally I don't. Where's the adventure in knowing exactly where you are *all* the time?

Allez, bonne promenade!

GLOSSARY

Throughout the text local words, either Breton or French, have been used to denote features whose character is peculiar to the area. Often there is no exact translation but the following is offered as a guide.

allée couverte - neolithic gallery grave

auberge - inn

balisage - way-marking

bourg - village with facilities

borne - boundary marker

château - castle or mansion

chemin creux - sunken track between raised banks

dolmen - ancient stone tomb

écluse - lock

étang - lake, usually artificial

fontaine - shrine over a spring

landes - high heathland, moor, with gorse and broom

La Poste - the post office

lavoir - old washing place

mairie - local government admin. office

marais - marsh

menhir - standing stone

métairie - tenanted farm

passerelle - footbridge

rigole - feeder channel

sentier - footpath

tourbière - peat bog

venelle - alleyway

VTT - mountain bike (*vélo tous terrains*)

La Fontaine de St-Bieuzy, Bieuzy

WALK 1: Ty Mat

Length 3¾kms	Time 1¼hrs	Level 2

Location & parking: from Hennebont, taking the D23 north through Lochrist (not the same as Inzinzac-Lochrist, which is nearby), pass through the village of Ty Flute and look for the 'parking randonnées' signed to the left. Park beside the avenue.

Refreshments: none on route.

A short walk with plenty of shade, ideal for a hot afternoon. The little river du Kersalo, where salmon spawn each winter, was dammed during WWII by the Germans to supply drinking water to their arsenal at Lorient. This walk takes a close look at the dam and passes around the resulting lake to return, with just a bit of a climb, past the entrance to the manoir of Ty Mat (chambres d'hôte).

DIRECTIONS

1. **From the top of the avenue, take the footpath sharp left, descending through the woods. Where the path forks, go right. At the road, bear right along it. After 100m turn left and cross the old concrete bridge. On the other side, take the track on the right between two banks. Where it climbs to the left to a crossroads of paths, follow it to the right.**
Passing through an open area, bear right downhill, and left at the water.

2. At the dam, follow the path as it zig-zags to a higher level. Continue alongside the lake. Where the track goes left uphill, take the path on the right to stay on the lakeside path or track.

3. At the road, turn right and cross the Red Bridge. Then turn right on the track.
Where the track goes left uphill, bear right through the barrier onto a narrow path, initially following the lake but soon bearing left uphill. At the top of the hill bear right along a path arriving from the left. Ignore another path arriving from the left and go straight on.
Bear left at two more paths joining from the right.
At the top of the hill go right and cross the road by the gates of the manoir, continuing ahead on the path.
Where another wide path arrives from the right, bear left along it to arrive at the starting point.

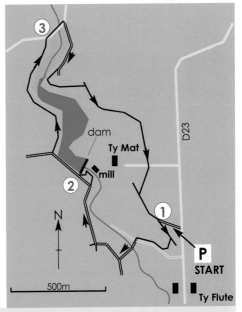

OTHER WALKS in the area:

This walk coincides with the *Circuit de la Forêt de Trémelin* (5km 2 hrs, waymarked green), which passes along the west side of the lake at Ty Mat. At the end of the lake turn left instead of right - the circuit returns to a point near the dam.

Inzinzac-Lochrist (3kms SW) *Mané Braz* 10kms 2½ hrs Start at Julien-le-Grand car-park (by the river). Waymarked yellow. This walk comes as far as the lake at Ty Mat.

Hennebont (8km S): *Circuit du Talhouët* 7km 2 hrs Start at TO in Hennebont. Waymarked green. Partly town, partly riverside. Details from the mairie 02 97 85 16 16 or TO 02 97 36 24 52

PLACES OF INTEREST nearby:

Hennebont (8kms S.): Haras National - everything you want to know about horses in Brittany.
http://www.haras-nationaux.fr

WALK 2: Forêt de Branguily

Length 5kms	Time 1½hrs	Level 2

Location & parking: 1km west of Gueltas, on the D125 Rohan to Pontivy. From Gueltas, park up the track on the left immediately after the *Déchetterie / Maison de l'Environnement*.

Refreshments: none on route.

This walk makes an ideal introduction to the tranquil delights of the Nantes - Brest Canal. For canal enthusiasts, there is the added attraction of the *Rigole d'Hilvern*.

After a walk along the Rigole the route descends by road to the canal, to return past a few of the ladder of locks that climbs up to the high point at Hilvern.

DIRECTIONS

1. From the car-park, cross to the north side of the D125 and go down the long, straight track.

Continue to the Nantes – Brest Canal and cross it by the bridge.

On the other side continue ahead away from the canal, follow the track round to the right, then take the path immediately on the left.

This path veers from side to side uphill for almost 500m, finally turning right at the top. From here the path goes straight, but leave it by turning left through a well-marked gap in the trees to reach the Rigole d'Hilvern.

The *Rigole d'Hilvern* is an artificial feeder channel that brought water from the barrage at Bosméléac, on the upper reaches of the Oust, to the canal at the high point of the plateau between the Oust and the Blavet. It has an incredibly long and tortuous route before joining the canal near Hilvern, just to the west of here. When it was first filled with water, very little of it actually reached the canal because of leakage. Today the canal is filled by a pumping station, and an association maintains the *rigole* and works for its rehabilitation.

2. Turn left along the Rigole and follow it for 1km as far as the road bridge.

Turn left on the road and walk down to the canal but do not cross it. Turn left along the towpath on the nearside of the canal.

Follow the towpath back to the bridge where you first crossed the canal and turn right over the bridge.

Retrace the track back to the D125 and the car park.

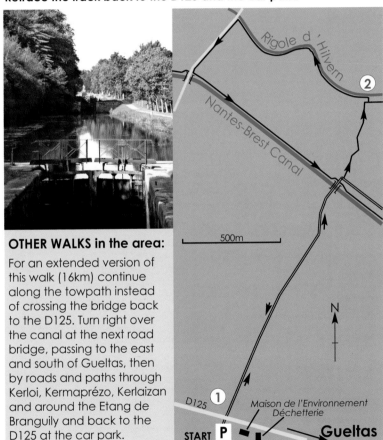

OTHER WALKS in the area:

For an extended version of this walk (16km) continue along the towpath instead of crossing the bridge back to the D125. Turn right over the canal at the next road bridge, passing to the east and south of Gueltas, then by roads and paths through Kerloi, Kermaprézo, Kerlaizan and around the Etang de Branguily and back to the D125 at the car park.

PLACES OF INTEREST nearby:

Maison de l'Environnement (also at 15 rue de l'Agrotte, Gueltas) open all year 9-12.30 & 2-6. Displays on nature conservation, waste disposal, wind farms, etc. Organised walks and field trips.
www.pontivy-communaute.fr

17

WALK 3: Lizio

Length 5kms	Time 1½hrs	Level 3

Location & parking: Lizio, 11kms south of Josselin. Park in the centre of the village.

Refreshments: in Lizio. None on route.

Lizio is a *'Petite Cité de Caractère'* with a pretty church in the centre and a few old buildings grouped around it. This walk begins in the village, then explores some of the wild wood and heathland to the north east, returning via *Le Val Jouin* with its two lakes. Near the end of this walk is the beginning of Lizio's *'sentier botanique'*, which, if taken in conjunction with this walk, would make a round circuit of 12kms.

DIRECTIONS

1. **From the west door of the church, take the road to the right, signed Josselin. Take the first road on the right. At the T-junction, continue ahead on a track into the wood.**

In a valley, the track narrows to a footpath, climbs, goes round to the right and down to meet another path arriving from the left. Follow this downhill to the right.

At the road, cross over, bearing left, and continue down the path opposite. After 100m go left and over the bank. Follow the path right and over another bank. Stay with the path uphill, round to the right, keeping within the woods. After snaking about in the wood, the path comes into a patch of gorse, then left over another bank into a pine wood. Here follow the beaten path through the pine trees, down through a clearing and over a little stream.

2. On the other side, where the path divides, turn sharp left and climb to more open woodland with gorse and small oak trees. Bear right where a path horseshoes in from the left, and bear left shortly afterwards. Where a path crosses, continue ahead on the main path ignoring others to either side.

Eventually emerging onto a straight track, follow this downhill to the right. At the bottom, over the stream, take the broad forest track on the right. Eventually the track follows the left side of a grassy valley with the stream meandering through it.

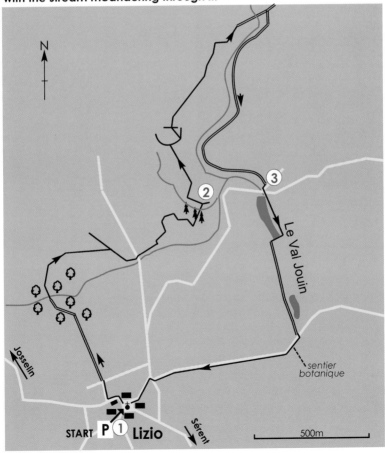

3. Turn right on the little road, then straight across the larger road a few metres later. Walk down through the car-park and continue on the grassy track to the left of the lake.

At the end of the lake cross over its barrage to the right, then left down the track. Follow this, past another lake, to the road. Here turn right.

(Note that after a few metres, on the left, a path leaves the road to embark upon the *Sentier Botanique*.)

Entering Lizio at the top of the road, cross the first road on the left and take the second, which leads into the centre of the village.

OTHER WALKS in the area:

Lizio: *Sentier Botanique* (7km). Trees and bushes are identified with information panels.

PLACES OF INTEREST nearby:

Lizio *L'Univers du Poète Ferrailleur* (World of the poet in scrap-iron) www.poeteferrailleur.com Open April - Oct Sundays and public holidays pm only, July to mid Sept every day am & pm.

Musée des Vieux Métiers (on the D174 to Quily, cross over the D4) Open Feb-Oct pm, April to Sept am & pm, Nov-Jan by appointment. 02 97 74 93 01 www.ecomuseelizio.com

Insectarium Live insects and exhibitions etc. Open Apr-Sept every day 10-6. 02 97 74 99 12

Sérent (5kms S) *Musée de Costumes Bretons* 9, rue du Pavé 56460 SERENT 02 97 75 93 77 Open July & August every afternoon, rest of year by appointment.

WALK 4: Auray - Town Walk

Length 6½kms	Time 2hrs	Level 2

Location & parking: the *Hotel de Ville*, *Place de la République*.
Park in the *Place de la République* or in any nearby car-park.

Refreshments: In Auray and at the port of St-Goustan.

This walk combines the old centre of Auray with the exceptionally picturesque port of Saint-Goustan. There are many interesting buildings along the way, including a look-out tower and the mausoleum of a famous Chouan leader, and fine waterside views along Le Loch estuary.

DIRECTIONS

1. Facing the town hall (*Hotel de Ville*), take a narrow passageway or *venelle* (marked Parc du Jeu de Paume) on the left. At the end turn right through the car-park. Straight ahead is the old prison.

This is actually a handsome building, renovated in the 1980s. Originally made a prison in 1788, it could house 90 inmates.

Facing the prison, turn right. Bear left at a junction, left again at a tiny square and then to the right along the Rue des Quatre Vents. Shortly after, turn right down a narrow passageway, the Venelle de St-Gildas. Then turn left up the Rue du Lait.

The Tourist Office, housed in an old chapel, is on the right hand side.

At the top of the road is the church.

The Eglise St-Gildas, a former priory that became the parish church, is a 17th century replacement of an earlier building.

From the church, cross the Place Notre Dame (a car-park) opposite and go through the narrow Rue J.Bernard (past a no entry sign) to the Chapelle du St-Esprit. Then take the road to the left of this (Rue des Fèves).

2. At the bottom, turn right and continue to the Chemin du Gaillec on the left. (NB - Ignore the Impasse du Gaillec – the pedestrian *Chemin* is a little further on.)

Follow the *chemin* down to the Chapelle St-Cadou and then

continue ahead, following the Rue du Reclus uphill. After 300m, turn left to the Mausolée de Cadoudal.

This is situated in the tiny hamlet of Kerléano – note the beautiful old houses beyond the mausoleum. Georges Cadoudal was born here, into a farming family, in 1771 – in the much updated *manoir* opposite the mausoleum. He became an important leader of the Chouan movement – Catholic royalist anti-revolutionaries who opposed the French Republic. He was arrested and guillotined in 1804. His bones were interred here and the mausoleum was completed in 1852.

3. **Walk diagonally across the park by the mausoleum, bear right at the narrow path and ahead at the road for about 80m to a T-junction. Here go left along the Boulevard Anne de Bretagne. Follow this sharp left soon after, then take the first right, Rue de Poul er Vran. At the end turn left, then right along the Rue des Chênes. Follow its 90° left bend, then turn right (Rue des Roses). At the end, go left and then immediately right (Rue St-Yves). Turn right at the end and follow this road to the end, where steps lead down past a pretty lavoir to the waterside.**

4. **Turn left, away from the motorway bridge, and walk for about a kilometre along Le Loch, which leads up to the ancient port of St-Goustan. Before the bridge, the ramparts of the old château estate are on the left. Climb the zig-zag path and steps here (excellent photos of the port possible), and then follow a narrow path left to**

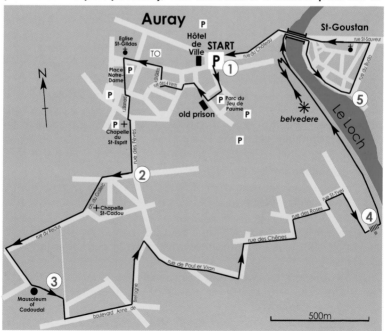

the look-out tower, which has open stairs to the top.

As early as 1644 a tower was positioned further downstream to give a strategic view over the entry to the port. This belvedere was rebuilt in 1721 further away to top the growing foliage along the steep banks of the estuary. The large open space here, now a sports ground, was once used for military exercises and fêtes.

Retrace your steps to the waterside and cross the bridge to the port.

There has been a bridge here since the 13th century, although the current one dates from 500 years later. St-Goustan was a port of great importance before the development of Lorient in the 18th century. Wine, salt, leather and iron were major imports, with significant quantities of grain, butter, fish and linen being exported.

Turn right along the waterfront for about 750m.

On the way, note the restaurant *Le Relais Franklin*, which has a plaque commemorating the 1776 arrival of the American who would later be president of the United States. He had made the 30 day journey across the Atlantic to seek the French king's support for the War of Independence from the British government.

5. Continue to the end of the quay by the little port office before turning uphill (Rue du Budo). At the top turn left along the rue du St-Sauveur towards the church.

Only the doorway remains from the original 15th century church, which was rebuilt after a fire in 1886. Next to it is the chapel of Notre Dame de Lourdes, a neo-gothic building from 1878, with an altarpiece recreating the grotto at Lourdes.

From the church take any of the narrow streets downhill to regain the port. Recross the bridge and bear left up the steep Rue du Château with its many attractive houses. At the top go straight ahead to reach the Hotel de Ville again.

OTHER WALKS in the area:

Auray The TO in Auray has three walks based on Auray; two of them are largely incorporated in this walk, the third starts from the *Place de la République* and explores the banks of Le Loch to the north of the town.

Bono (5km SE) 'Two rivers and the ocean' - 8.3kms 2¾hrs Start at the *Place de la Mairie* car-park, Bono, passing the bridges over the river Bono, the Tumulus of Kernours (take a torch to see inside) and the Château de Kerdréan (13th-16th century, now a hotel).

PLACES OF INTEREST nearby:

Ste-Anne d'Auray (5kms NE) an elaborate church, which is a major centre of pilgrimage with a pardon on 26th July, and a WW1 memorial. Also the *Historial - Musée de Cire* (waxworks museum). www.musee-de-cire.com

WALK 5: Ploërmel - Town Walk

Length 6½kms	Time 2hrs	Level 1

Location & parking: picnic area near the D766E exit from the N24. Alternative start: town centre.

Refreshments: plenty of choice.

This walk combines the historic centre of Ploërmel, a very interesting town of many fine buildings, with a more rural stroll along an old railway line. The latter runs near the express way, so it is a pretty, but not silent, route, providing easy walking in pleasant countryside. Varied architecture includes the old defences, historic houses and an astronomical clock.

DIRECTIONS

1. From the picnic area by the D766E, near the express way, double back under the main road on an old railway line. This track lined with oaks at first runs parallel with the express way, 400m away.

Cross straight over at the next road junction.

Continue to the busy D766, cross and follow the track ahead.

The 15th century *Chapelle St-Antoine* is visible off to the left across the express way – a pedestrian *passerelle* provides access.

At the next little road, cross straight over and follow the grassed area ahead or the tarmac road running parallel.

2. At the top, bear right on the track. This comes out on a small road, with a red-earthed footpath by it. Bear right along it and continue ahead for 450m. At the end, bear right to the roundabout. Cross the first road to the right and head up the *Rue de la Gare* (signed *Centre Ville*). At the top, turn left along the *Rue du Val*. Continue past the Tourist Office on the left to the *Chapelle Sainte Marie des Carmes*.

Often called the 'Blue Chapel' from its unusual windows, this building dates from the late 19th century. Today it is used mainly for exhibitions and cultural events. The original convent here was founded in 1273 and remains of the old cloisters can be seen off the *Boulevard des Carmes* (when redevelopment work for the creation of a new mediathèque permits).

Cross the *Rue du Val* directly in front of the chapel towards the car-park – note the remnants of the ancient town walls dating from the 12th century, above and ahead. **Take the first narrow street to the right, *Rue des Fosses.***

In a little square, bear ahead right along the *Rue du Duc de Mercoeur*. Ahead, a large church is visible across another car-park. Cross to the church and go round to the left of it, and under an arch, following signs to the astronomical clock.

This remarkable clock, to be found in a huge glass case in the cloister of this former abbey, was constructed between 1850 and 1855 by Frère Bernardin. There is an information board in English, and a small museum nearby exhibits the work of Jean-Marie de la Mennais, an educationally influential priest and writer (1780-1860).

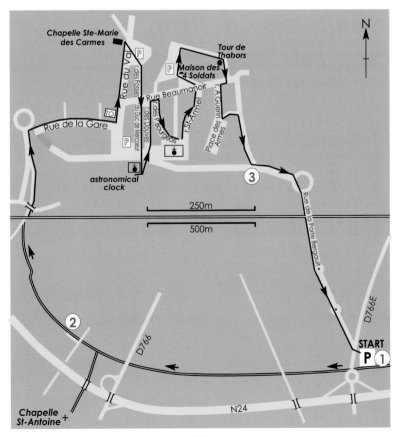

Re-cross the road, bear right towards the main church but before then go left down the *Rue des Douves*. Turn right at the bottom between two superb historic houses.

The *Maison des Marmousets*, with its fine carvings, dates from the 16th century, whilst the mainly 15th century *Maison des Ducs de Bretagne* is the oldest building in the town, with parts going back to the 12th century.

Turn first right into the *Rue des Francs Bourgeois* and follow it up to the church.

The gothic style Church of St-Armel contains many impressive details, including early stained glass windows (e.g. a Tree of Jesse from 1552) and the joint tomb of two dukes of Brittany, Jean II and III. The north door is architecturally striking, as is the 18th century square bell-tower.

Leave the church by the same door, and bear right and then left (before the archway) down the narrow *Rue St Armel*.

Just before the bottom on the right is the *Ancienne Hotel de la Monnaie*, with its five storey stair tower, dating back to medieval times.

At the end of the road bear left and ahead across a little square. On the right is the *Maison des Quatre Soldats*, a remarkable building now housing a café/tabac. In the car-park behind this building bear right and continue round past the old stone tower.

The *Tour de Thabors* is the only remaining tower of the original town fortifications, which enclosed the oldest part of the town.

Turn right at the road junction, then left down *Rue Alphonse Guerin*. In *Places des Armes* go up the steps to the left, beyond the memorial, then turn right down to the main road.

3. Turn left here. In 200m at a roundabout, turn right. Follow this residential road (*Rue de la Porte Bergault*) for 400m. At a mini-roundabout, bear left. Continue ahead through the new estate, across another mini-roundabout, and down across the D766 to return to the picnic/parking area.

OTHER WALKS in the area:

Ploërmel *Chemin des Hortensias* 7kms 2hrs Start from the old railway station in Ploërmel. Passes by the *Lac au Duc* and includes the *sentier botanique des Hortensias*.

St-Maudé (9km E, to the north of the N24) *Circuit de St-Maudé* 9kms 2¼ hrs, via the villages of La Croix-Hélléan and Hélléan. (See *Central Brittany Coast to Coast*, walk 11.)

Guillac (6kms SW) *Circuit des Croix* 13kms 3½ hrs Start from the Moulin de Guillac on the Nantes-Brest Canal. Passes wayside crosses, a fontaine and the parish church of Guillac.

WALK 6: Rochefort-en-Terre

Length 6kms	Time 1½hrs	Level 2

Location & parking: Rochefort-en-Terre, just north of the D775 Vannes to Redon. Park near Place St-Michel or Champ de Foire, at the east end of town. (In high season, if parking is difficult, the walk could be started from any point in the town centre or by the lake, *Etang du Moulin Neuf*.)

Refreshments: plenty of choice in Rochefort, otherwise the *Centre des Vacances* at *Le Moulin Neuf*.

Rochefort-en-Terre well merits its title *Petite Cité de Caractère*. In the summer the streets throng with visitors and the beauty of the old houses is complemented by the brilliance of the floral displays, mostly geraniums, for which the town is famous. This walk takes a tour around the outside of the town and returns to the town centre from the south, passing the church, la Collègiale, and climbing to the main thoroughfares, from which one can either return to the car-park by the most direct route, or explore the *venelles* and back streets.

DIRECTIONS

1. From Place St-Michel take the D774, direction Malestroit. Go through Le Vieux Bourg (old town) down into the valley. There are some beautiful old houses either side of this road, built of the local shist with granite embellishments.

At the bottom of the hill take the 'no through road' on the left. At its end, continue ahead on the footpath and carry on for about 1km.

Initially this is like a *chemin creux* formed by a stone wall on the left and the steep hillside on the right but soon it becomes an open path through the wood, along the bottom of the valley. The remains of a slate fence line the path on the left - a fairly constant theme through much of this walk – using the readily available local material, but many of the slates have holes punched through them, suggesting the re-use of roofing slates.

2. At a farm on the right, take the little road on the left. Cross the river, then take the footpath immediately on the right. This climbs slightly following the line of the trees and another slate fence on the right.

At a road, cross straight over and carry on up the path.

Across another road, continue on the track ahead. Ignore a track arriving from the left (except to go up it for a few metres to see the Moulin de Bogeäis - a windmill converted into a house - and return to your original path).

Continue ahead down the hill. At a confusion of paths, with the lake visible through the trees to the right, go straight ahead. The path bears right and soon descends to the track encircling the lake.

Detour: turn right and go right around the lake to rejoin the walk at Point No.4 (2.3km).

3. Turn left and follow the path over a bridge into the complex of the Moulin Neuf (New Mill, but looking very old and derelict now. The further part of this complex has been converted into a *Centre des*

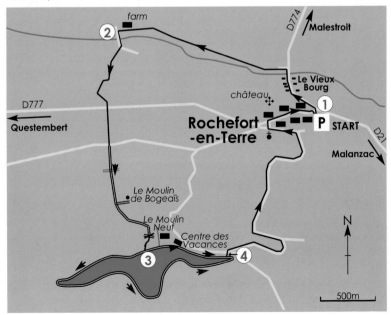

Vacances) – walk along the quay to the right of the *Centre des Vacances*, then continue on the lakeside path.

4. At the flight of steps on the left, almost at the end of the lake, climb to the road, cross and go up the road opposite. At the top turn left and follow this road back into Rochefort.

The road enters the town at the bottom, crossing over a little river where there are some old sheltered lavoirs down on the right.

Passing under a stone arch, go left up the road to see the church. Continue uphill to the main street, turning right here to go through the town centre to the car-park.

OTHER WALKS in the area:

Rochefort : the TO has details of a longer version of this walk, taking in a wider circuit to the north.

PLACES OF INTEREST nearby:

Rochefort-en-Terre *Château* - dating from the 12th century, purchased in 1907 by American portraitist Alfred Klots, now the property of the Conseil General de Morbihan. Open in April at week-ends 2.00-6.30; in May at week-ends and public holidays 2.00-6.30; June & Sept every day 2.00-6.30; July/Aug every day 10.00-6.30.

TO Rochefort-en-Terre, place des Halles. 02.97.43.33.57. www.rochefort-en-terre.com

Le Guerno (19kms S) *Parc Animalier et Botanique de Branféré* Almost 1,000 animals of over 120 species cohabit freely in a park of 40 hectares. Open Feb to Nov. 02 97 42 94 66 www.branfere.com

Malansac (5kms SE) *Parc de Prehistoire de Bretagne* - from dinosaurs to man. 02 97 43 34 17

WALK 7: Guémené - the upper Scorff

Length 7½kms	Time 2hrs	Level 2

Location & parking: north of Guémené-sur-Scorff. Take the D3 towards Rostrenen and park in the first lay-by (approx. 400m).

Refreshments: none on route - plenty in Guémené.

The upper reaches of the river Scorff are noted for their quiet and verdant beauty. This route sets out along the river past a couple of former mills before climbing to explore the wider countryside, then crossing the river to return along the opposite slopes of the valley. Most of the route is shady so the walk would be a good choice for a hot day.

DIRECTIONS

1. From the lay-by take the track that descends to a bridge over the river. Cross over and bear left along the path rising into the woods above the 'private' garden of the Moulin à Tan. Once past the Moulin à Tan, descend to the larger path along the riverbank and continue to the next mill, Moulin de Nicol.

Where the path divides, bear left across three little bridges (over a tributary to the Scorff). The path now climbs (ignore the path to the right) to follow the tree-lined boundary between two fields. At the road turn left.

2. At the T-junction (the hamlet of Kergrahouahic to the right) cross to the path opposite. Continue up through woodland, then between fields. Emerging onto the sparsely wooded hillside, pass through a bank to the left and bear right to follow the track, descending to the village of Quénépèvan.

3. Turn left at the road and left again at the main road. After 300m turn left onto a track. Follow this straight up and over the hill, then down through pasture to farm buildings on the right. Continue on the road to the bottom of the hill. Here turn right at the T-junction. Cross the river and continue up to the D3.

4. Cross to the gap in the trees and footpath on the opposite side of the D3. After 50m turn left along another path running parallel with the road.

Passing above the hamlet of Poulhibet, bear right along a track coming up from the road.

Follow this track for about 1km, continuing when it becomes a grassy path and descending straight on down to join the road that serves *gîtes* overlooking the D1/D3 junction. Continue down to the D1, turning left to the junction, and there go left on the D3 for the 400m back to the starting point.

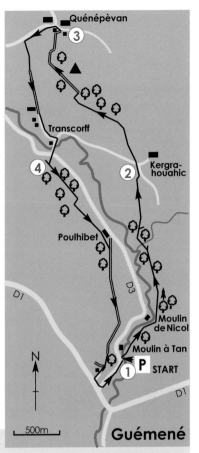

Guémené

OTHER WALKS in the area:

Guémené: *Boucle de Krenenan* - 11km country walk, taking in the chapel and fontaine of Krenenan.

Valley of the Scorff: a route follows the river Scorff from its source near Mellionec in Côtes d'Armor to Quéven, near Lorient. There are several circuits from this and more are being added. Leaflets are available from TOs and mairies in the valley or from the Maison du Scorff, Bas-Pont-Scorff, 56620 Cléguer 02 97 32 50 79 syndicat-scorff@wanadoo.fr

Lignol (7.5kms SW) *Circuit de Mari Chôn* (legendary Lignol character) 10kms. Countryside, villages, chapel of St-Yves and remains of Mari Chôn's house.

PLACES OF INTEREST NEARBY:

Guémené the *Rohan Gate*, which is all that remains of the château. Other interesting old buildings in the town.

Length 8½kms	Time 2½hrs	Level 3/4

Location & parking: Le Faouët on the D769, 15km S of Gourin, 32km N of Lorient. Park by the market hall in the centre.

Refreshments: in Le Faouët or at Chapelle St-Barbe in high season.

The market town of Le Faouët in western Morbihan is known for its 17th century Market Hall and for two remarkable chapels, one of which is included on this walk. Less well-known are the remains of the Château de Barrégan, a 13th century feudal castle overlooking the valley of the river Ellé. The route of this walk passes the château before descending to the river and following its 'chaos' for over a kilometre. The chapel of Ste-Barbe and its associated fontaine are a delight that is saved for near the end of the walk.

DIRECTIONS

1. From the upper side of the Market Hall (Les Halles), cross the street and take the Rue des Halles opposite. At the end of the street, cross over and continue ahead downhill. This road soon becomes a track, then a broad path down through the woods. At the bottom, turn left by the stump of an old stone cross (do not go through the underpass).

At the road, turn right and under the bridge. Immediately on the other side, take the path on the left that climbs parallel with the main road for 100m, before turning to the right and up a broad woodland track later narrowing to a path. Bear left uphill at a stony road, cross the tarmac road and continue up the stony track opposite.

2. At the metal gates, bear left on the footpath. Follow this ancient path down the hillside. At a larger path, turn left. Turn right onto the road in the village of Villeneuve Barrégan. At the end of the road, continue ahead uphill (ignoring the track descending to the right).

Where the path bends left and goes along the left hand edge of a wood, there are the remains of a castle 50m to the right, hidden in the woods. The 13th century Château de Barrégan was the property of the Lords of Le Faouët in 1390. From 1426 it was superseded by a manor house. It is possible to walk around the outer rampart to the right and then onto the central mound from the other side.

Returning to the path, continue as before, turning right downhill to stay within the woods, then left. Where the path descends, within sight of a house on the opposite hillside, the remains of a *fontaine* and *lavoir* (but very overgrown at the time of writing) can be found under a large tree ahead, where the path turns right.

At a T-junction of paths, turn left up to the road. Here turn left. Where the road bends left at the top of the hill, take the footpath straight ahead.

3. 100m after entering the wood, turn right onto a footpath through the pine trees. At a bluff above the river, the path turns right and descends to the level of the river and runs along outside the bottom of the woods.

At a road by a water station, turn right and, with the building on your left, turn left on a broad, straight path into the pine wood. At the river, ignore the bridge ahead and continue to the right, downstream (beware, the tree roots can be slippery).

After a while the path climbs to a rocky viewpoint overlooking the valley, descending again steeply to the river bank and continuing downstream.

4. After about 1km, where the river bank becomes a little less wooded, take the path on the right. This emerges after 50m onto a bracken covered hillside, crosses another path coming up from the river, and continues steeply uphill to the Fontaine Ste-Barbe. Climb to the left of the fontaine and, crossing over another wide path, mount the roughly paved path (an ancient pilgrim path) that goes up the hillside to the left. At the top is the chapel of Ste-Barbe.

The Chapelle de Ste-Barbe was built in the late 15th century by Jean de Toulbodou who, whilst hunting at this spot, was miraculously saved from falling rocks when lightning struck the cliff-face above him. (Ste-Barbe is frequently associated with lightning and is the patron saint of firemen as well as slate-workers.) The chapel contains some fine early 16th century stained glass, and is reached from above by a magnificent baroque staircase.

Climb up all the steps, coming out at the top onto a grassy plateau with an _auberge_ (possibility of refreshments in season) on the right. Go straight ahead through the gap in the perimeter wall and straight on over the hill, descending into the trees along another pilgrim path with, eventually, a bee museum (_musée de l'abeille vivante_) on the left. Cross over the little road, down the steps and through the underpass. On the other side is the base of a stone cross seen on your outward route. Retrace your steps back to the start.

OTHER WALKS in the area:

Le Faouët _Circuit des Chapelles,_ 12kms 3½ hrs, including Ste-Barbe (seen on this walk) and St-Fiacre with its restored painted rood screen. A variant of this circuit is the _Balade au Pays de la Marion_, based on a famous 18th century female bandit who operated in the area.

Gourin (10kms NW) _Circuit des Ardoisiers._ 13kms 3½ hrs Starts from the Château de Tronjoly and passes several former slate quarries.

PLACES OF INTEREST nearby:

La Chapelle de St-Fiacre (2kms S of Le Faouët) Restored polychrome rood screen and other religious carvings in stone and wood.

WALK 9: Ménéac

Length 7½kms	Time 2hrs	Level 2

Location & parking: Bellouan. From the centre of Ménéac take the D305, direction Illifaut, take the first right after the Ménéac exit sign and park on the verge.

Refreshments: in Ménéac. None on route.

Admirers of menhirs will love this one, but its setting is unusual - the depression in the ground around its base gives it the appearance of a whale coming up for air - it's certainly a powerful image.
The walk also takes in an old mill, several farms and affords a glimpse of the early 17th century chapel in the private grounds of the Manoir de Bellouan.

DIRECTIONS

1. Continue down the road to a sign on the left to the 'Menhir de Bellouan'. Take the footpath indicated, through the trees for 300m to the menhir.

From the menhir, continue between the trees for a further 50m, then side step to the left, outside the trees, to follow the edge of the field. Go ahead through the hedgerow to a grassy area with rocks and artificial lakes etc. (Private land - please keep to the path.) **Keep to the right of the area and pass to the right of the lakes.**

Where the path meets a track, go left. Follow the track round to the left and up to the road.

Here turn right along the road. Continue for 500m past La Veria, ignoring the left turn to La Maudué. Where the road reaches the trees, take the track on the left. Follow it for 1km, ignoring a track on the left, and turn right at the road.

Follow the road for 500m to where it bends right: here take the track on the left. Bear right after 300m, and at the houses take the track to the left.

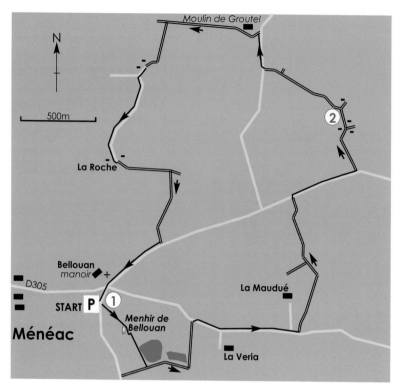

2. **After 100m turn left onto a track bordering a field. Bear right with the track. Ignore the track on the right at the top of the rise - continue down to the road and turn right.**

In the valley turn left (signed 'Groutel').

The Moulin de Groutel is on the right almost immediately. An old mill-stone rests under a tree, and another lies on the other side of the building, beyond which the leet now flows through an open sluice.

Continue on the track for 500m, then take the track on the left. In a hamlet the track becomes a road. At the T-junction go left.

Follow the road down to La Roche and continue ahead on the track. Follow this right, ignoring a grassy track ahead. At the road turn right and follow it for 500m, past the gates of the Manoir de Bellouan and its chapel, to the junction near the start of the walk.

OTHER WALKS in the area:

Brignac (6km SE): *Circuit de St-Barthélémy* 12kms 3 hrs, but much of it is road walking.

WALK 10: Peillac

Length 8kms	Time 2hrs	Level 2

Location & parking: Peillac, on the D764 between Malestroit and Redon. From Peillac take the D14 towards Les Fougerêts for 1.2kms, park on the right by the canal.

Refreshments: *auberge* near car-park, otherwise in Peillac.

The Nantes to Brest canal is a recurring theme for walkers in Morbihan. It often affords the most strikingly beautiful scenery but no two stretches of the canal are ever the same. Its character subtly changes as it traverses the department from Redon to Pontivy. In this walk we follow it eastwards along a section of the River Oust on the edge of low lying country, cross the canal where it diverges from the river, explore some reclaimed marshland and re-cross the canal at a spectacular tree-lined cut. The return journey follows the wooded hillside just south of the canal, taking in a pretty village, a couple of small lakes and a converted windmill.

DIRECTIONS

1. From the car-park by the canal follow the towpath to the right all the way to the first lock, No.20 the *Ecluse de Limur*.

On the way look out for the Barge de Boissel, which is a branch of the canal leaving at right-angles from the opposite bank. This would have served as an access to the cultivated marshland between the canal, here formed by the river Oust, and the Ruisseau des Fougerêts. The canal facilitated the delivery of fertilizer and the transport of farm produce. The *Ecluse de Limur* marks the point where the canal from Redon rejoins the river Oust after

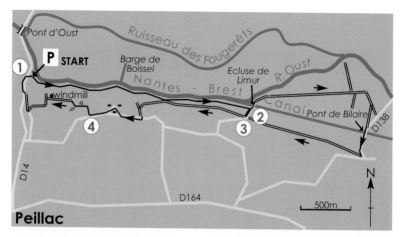

Peillac

passing through a straight trench for about 5kms. The totally different character of this cut canal can be seen from the bridge over the lock.

2. **(Possibility of a shorter walk at this point by turning right up the road for a few metres to point 3)**

Cross over the lock by the bridge and follow the track ahead. Bear right on the track and continue straight ahead for about 1km. Soon after the track bends right, take the right fork. Bear right on the D138 to cross the canal by the *Pont de Bilaire*. Continue to the junction and here take the <u>first</u> road on the right, soon becoming a track. Follow this for several hundred metres.

3. Where the track crosses a road, continue ahead on the track. At a point passed on the outward route within a few metres of the canal, continue on the track, bearing left to another track coming up from the right. Bear left up to the road. Here turn right and take the first road on the right through a hamlet with some attractive houses, following the road left and down to rejoin the main road.

4. After 120m take the footpath on the right down the far side of a field. Follow the path into the wood, passing to the left of a small lake. Bear right uphill at another lake on the left. Note the old stone windmill in the trees on the right.

At a T-junction of tracks, turn left, following the track to the right around a garden. Where the track bends left and becomes a tarmac road, turn sharp right onto the track that descends to another road. Bear right here down to the car-park.

OTHER WALKS in the area:

Pont d'Oust (where the D14 crosses the canal - see map)
Le Sentier des Châtaigniers (the chestnut path): start at the *Pont d'Oust* - about an hour's walk.

WALK 11: Plouay

Length 8kms	Time 2hrs	Level 3

Location & parking: Plouay, just east of the D769, 20kms north of Lorient. Park near the Tourist Office or Champion supermarket.

Refreshments: in Plouay - none on route.

The town of Plouay has made a name for itself as a centre of cycling. The Vélodrome is part of a complex that includes a museum of cycling. Cycling as a sport, by its very nature, cannot be contained within the Véloparc and often spills out into the surrounding countryside with organised road races and VTT events.

DIRECTIONS

1. **Make for the Champion supermarket (visible from the TO). Go left along the track that runs behind the supermarket.**

Follow the track ahead into woods and past a no-entry sign with a house on the left. Ignore other tracks and paths joining from either side. After 1km look out for a path on the left leading down to the *Fontaine de Stang Philippe* (20m). Return to the track. Continue to the road and turn left. Turn right again almost immediately. Follow this road for more than 1km through the village of Nézerh, where the tarmac ends.

2. **Continue ahead on a cart-track. Where the track divides, go right, then left when it divides again, taking the path along the edge of the wood. Down in the dip take the footpath on the right - into the wild, natural forest. Ignore a path joining from the right after a few hundred metres.**

3. **At a T-junction of paths turn right downhill. (The river Scorff is now**

Fontaine de Stang Philippe

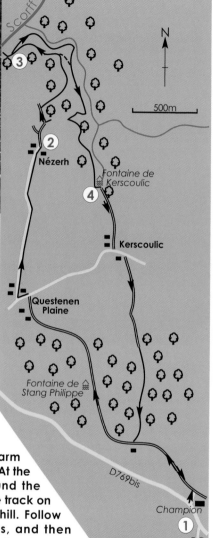

below on your left, but following the path, you will soon realise you are walking up a tributary of the Scorff. Soon a path joins from the right - this is the one you ignored earlier).

After a while the path climbs to the right and then levels to the left, eventually looping left around a natural (minus the customary stonework) spring - the *Fontaine de Kerscoulic*.

4. Leave the spring by the farm track up to Kerscoulic village. At the road turn left, then just around the slight right-hand bend take the track on the right, going gently downhill. Follow this track up into the woods, and then ahead on the path, descending to arrive back on your outward route near the house by the no-entry sign. Turn left to return to Plouay.

PLACES OF INTEREST nearby:

Plouay *Véloparc*, a space entirely devoted to the bicycle, includes a museum. Open all year: June-Sept every day 10-7, Oct-May closed Mon and Sun am and lunchtimes. Domaine de Ménéhouarne, 56240 Plouay. 02 97 33 15 15

WALK 12: St-Pierre-Quiberon & the Côte Sauvage

Length 8kms	Time 2hrs	Level 2

Location & parking: St-Pierre-Quiberon, which is just past the Penthièvre isthmus on the D768. Car-park next to the Tourist Information point in the town centre.

Refreshments: in Portivy and St-Pierre Quiberon.

The Quiberon Peninsula is one of those places that cannot fail to fascinate, just by its shape on the map - a long finger of land pointing into the Atlantic. The east side is sheltered and normally calm, the west side takes the full force of the ocean and is not for nothing called *le Côte Sauvage* - the wild coast. Neolithic man has left his mark, and there are also remains from the Iron Age. The peninsula was an easy target for raiders. The English pillaged the chapel of Notre-Dame de Lotivy in 1746 (War of the Austrian Succession) and in 1795 landed a force of French royalists on the peninsula. Unfortunately that was where they stayed, bottled up by the French Republican army under General Hoche. This walk passes dolmens, the chapel, the little harbour at Portivy and takes in a good stretch of the *Côte Sauvage*.

DIRECTIONS

1. **Across the road from the car-park, take the footpath ahead, following it through to the main road. Over the zebra-crossing bear right up the *Chemin de la Fontaine*, parallel with the main road. At the end, continue ahead to the road and turn left. 100m before the mini-roundabout, look for the *Rue du Dolmen* on the right.**

41

This village is called Le Roch after the dolmen, which is an unusually large, round, neolithic burial chamber, looking a bit like a tortoise. Round chambers such as this are not common.

2. Continue straight on at the mini-roundabout, across the level crossing and bear right. After the first road on the left, take the track on the right towards the windmill. At the end, continue ahead on the path. At the road turn left, then bear left at the chapel.

The *Chapelle de Notre-Dame de Lotivy* was originally constructed in the 11th century on the site of an oratory dedicated to the Welsh saint David. It was pillaged by the English during the War of the Austrian Succession in 1746 and after the Revolution it was just a ruin. In 1844/5 it was rebuilt (at the request of the Virgin, through the medium of a local girl).

Deviation: below the chapel, take the little road to the right to see the *Fontaine de Lotivy*. Built about 1700 and said to be where St-David, or perhaps one of his disciples, quenched his thirst, it was part of the old priory of Lotivy. According to local tradition, its waters can cure colic in infants and strengthen their limbs.

From the chapel, continue down to the junction and turn right. Bear right at the mini-roundabout and follow the road through to the harbour.

Turn left along the quay and follow the coast path. Passing behind the *Plage du Foso*, (pausing to see the memorial dedicated to American mothers), continue out to the point.

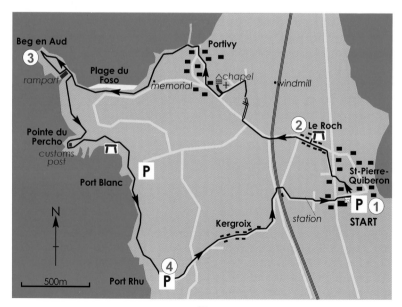

On the way to the point, Beg en Aud, look out for the very large rampart that towers above the coast path. This served to defend an Iron Age village. In the 1st century BC, there was a fortified camp of the Venetes tribe here. From the point there is an almost 360° view over the Plage de Foso, Portivy, the Fort de Penthièvre, the coast round to Lorient and the Île de Groix; then to the left there is the tip of Belle Île, La Pointe des Poulains.

3. Continuing on from Beg en Aud, the path returns to the end of the rampart. Here turn right to retrace your steps for a few metres before turning sharp right to continue on the coast path southwards.

At the next point, Pointe du Percho, there is a former customs post. Continue on, past an excavated dolmen on the clifftop to the right, to Port Blanc (marked by an orange telephone and a car-park). Here, depending on the tide and the weather, you can see the granite arch of Port Blanc. Continue along the coast.

4. At Port Rhu (again marked by an orange telephone and a car-park) turn left inland through the car-park. Go ahead at the crossroads and left at the fork, into Kergroix. Follow the street left and up to the main road. Here bear left and over the level crossing. Bear right, behind the station.

Follow this road ahead. Cross the main road and continue ahead, to the left of the *Centre Culturel*, **to find the Tourist Information point and the car-park.**

OTHER WALKS in the area:

Quiberon The TO in St-Pierre-Quiberon will be able to provide details of other walks on the peninsula.

Carnac (13½km N) *Tro Braz* 18km 5hrs Start at the *Salle des Fêtes*, Menac. A circuit around the major neolithic and later sites of the Carnac area.

PLACES OF INTEREST nearby:

St-Pierre-Quiberon *Cromlech of St-Pierre-Quiberon* and *Alignments of St-Pierre-Quiberon* - evidence of neolithic occupation of Quiberon.

Plouharnel (8km N) *Musée de la Chouanerie* (on the road to Quiberon, in a bunker by a level crossing) Excellent museum dedicated to the Breton anti-republican, royalist, Catholic movement of the Chouans.

Quiberon (5km S) Town and harbour - boats to Belle Île, Houat and Hoëdic.

Carnac (13½km N) Neolithic alignments certainly, but don't miss the Tumulus of Kercado (by the *Château de Kercado*, off the D196) or Carnac's *Musée de Préhistoire*.

WALK 13: Béganne - Port de Foleux

Length 9kms	Time 2½hrs	Level 2

Location & parking: Port de Foleux, signed from the D20 Muzillac to Redon, near Béganne. Park opposite the bar/crêperie.

Refreshments: in Port Foleux, none on route.

The port of Foleux is a staging post and anchorage for pleasure boats navigating the River Vilaine between Redon and La Roche-Bernard downstream. The walk sets out from the port, and by roads and tracks follows the river upstream, crossing the cultivated marshland beyond Le Ruaud before climbing to a return route with many good views across the river. The final part, which can be left out if desired, explores the hills behind the port and village of Foleux, returning down the valley of the Rivière de l'Étier.

DIRECTIONS

1. From the car-park behind the crêperie, take the road to the left (east), parallel with the river, eventually turning inland to a junction. Here bear right into the village of Brédan. At the crossroads in Brédan, turn right. Follow this road around a few bends to the ruined chapel of St-Cado.

2. Bear left on the footpath around the end of the chapel, then turn right to cross the stream by a footbridge. At the road turn left and take the first road on the right. Through Le Ruaud, continue ahead on the long, straight track across the marshes. At a T-junction turn

left, go over the bridge and where the road begins to climb, take the track on the right. Follow the track uphill to join the road at a crossroads. Here turn left.

3. Bear right at the fork, ignore the next road on the left and bear right up to a T-junction with a cross on the right. Here turn left.

Bear left at the next fork and follow the road downhill, past Grand Brécéan, through Le Verger, and down to Cado. (Fine views across the River Vilaine.) At the crossroads in Cado continue ahead, and follow the road to a triangular junction. Turn left to reach Brédan. At the crossroads in Brédan (same crossroads as on your outward route) turn right up the track.

4. At the top of the hill, take the footpath on the right going towards the trees. Once in the wood the path wanders to the other side and eventually emerges at the edge of a field by a noticeboard advertising the Château de Léhelec and its museum. Here bear left back into the woods on a grassy track.

On reaching the road, turn left. After 100m take the track on the right, descending quite steeply. At the bottom, bear left and go down the steps to visit a *fontaine* and *lavoir*, returning up the steps afterwards and continuing on the track to the right that skirts the top edge of the valley (ignoring the track down into the valley).

Over the crest of the hill, bear right with the track to pass along the bottom of the valley. The path then turns sharply left, still within the trees, and goes through a narrow wooden barrier. Follow the path through another barrier and onto the track below, turning left along it. Follow this track all the way to the Port of Foleux, here bearing left to find the car-park.

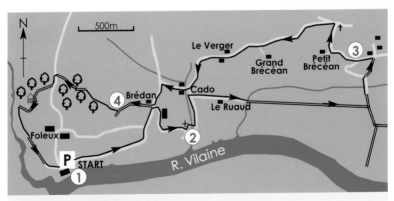

PLACES OF INTEREST nearby:

Château de Léhélec Béganne 02 99 91 84 33 Guided visits 1st Jul - 1st Sep every day except Tuesday.

WALK 14: Erdeven megaliths

Length 9½kms	Time 3hrs	Level 2

Location & parking: Erdeven, on the D781 between Belz and Plouharnel/Carnac. Park in the car-park for the *Alignements de Kerzerho*, just east of Erdeven on the D781.

Refreshments: In Erdeven, none on route.

Cromlech of Crucuno

This walk is mostly on well-maintained woodland tracks, and takes in an amazing variety of megalithic architecture. So numerous are the menhirs and dolmens that afterwards one imagines seeing them everywhere and every heap of rocks in a hedgerow raises the question - is it a dolmen? Could it possibly have been overlooked?

DIRECTIONS

1. **From the car-park explore the alignments of Kerzerho.** These are the westernmost alignments of the Carnac group, 195 megaliths in 5 rows, but unfortunately the road has displaced some of them.

From a corner of the area, near the car-park, a footpath leaves towards the 'Géants de Kerzerho'. This path shortly emerges in a series of little glades, each containing its own collection of giant stones, some standing, some lying, and with several smaller stones dotted around. **Continue through the stones to a T-junction of paths and turn right, signed Mané Braz.**

2. **Where the path joins a track, follow it to the right.** There are many hundreds of megaliths dotted around the pine woods and fields that border this wide, sandy track. **Ignore any side tracks and continue to a crossroads of tracks.**

3. Crossing straight over, continue to a T-junction of tracks and turn right. Shortly, a path on the left leads uphill to Mané Braz, where there are four neolithic burial sites. The first is a dolmen comprising an entrance passage leading to four separate chambers. The second dolmen has just a single chamber and the remaining two smaller dolmens have lost most of their roof stones.

Return down the hill (there is a line of megaliths on the opposite side of the path) **and turn left to continue the walk.**

4. After 200m, take the track on the left signed to Mané Croc'h. At a junction of tracks turn right, still following signs to Mané Croc'h. After 150m, opposite a seat, take the path on the left to Caesar's Chair. This is another alignment but Caesar's chair is unmistakable. **Return to the main path, turning left, and continue to a car-park.**

5. From the car-park there is a path to the right that leads down to the lake (herons, sea-gulls and other bird-life), and a path to the left that leads up to the dolmen, Mané Croc'h, beside the road. **Follow the road to the right to the village of Crucuno.**

6. Follow the road round to the left to see a massive dolmen beside a house. The roof stone at an estimated 60 tonnes is the heaviest known.

Take the road to the left of the house by the dolmen and continue ahead where it becomes a track. After 350m take the track on the

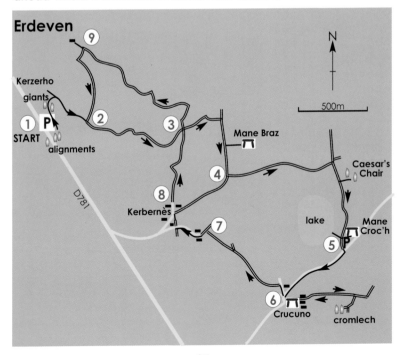

Crucuno dolmen

right. In 100m, where the track bends left, take the track on the right that leads up to a square of megaliths - the Cromlech of Crucuno.

Return to point 6. and the beginning of the road by which you arrived in Crucuno, cross it and take the road that forks left of the modern house. After 100m take the earth road descending to the left and follow it, swinging right uphill between fields. Where it divides, bear left and continue on the grassy track.

7. At the T-junction go left. At the houses go right on the tarmac road and follow it round to the left. At a crossroads of tracks in 50m take the track on the right and continue ahead on the path through trees. At the road, ignore another track arriving from the right and go ahead up the road (signed Erdeven).

8. The road becomes a track, leading to the crossroads of tracks at point 3 on your outward walk. Here go straight on, signed Keraveon. Continue on this track, ignoring signs to Kercadio.

9. When a house comes into view ahead, turn left (signed Kerzerho) and, following the path to the junction at point 2, turn right to repeat in reverse the first part of the walk back to the car-park.

Mané Croc'h

PLACES OF INTEREST nearby:

Carnac (9km SE) Visit the world-famous alignments of menhirs lying just to the north and east of the town, but don't miss the *Musée de Préhistoire* in the town centre - a major collection of neolithic material well presented. Open Jul/Aug every day 10-6: May/Jun/Sept 10-12.30 & 2-6: Oct-Apr 10-12.30 & 2-5. (Sept-Jun closed Tuesdays, Wednesday mornings in Jan, 1st May & 25th Dec.)

WALK 15: Inguiniel

Length 9½kms	Time 3hrs	Level 2

Location & parking: Inguiniel, 10kms from Plouay on the D18 to Guémené-sur-Scorff. Park in the car-park by the church.

Refreshments: none on route.

This walk takes you from the sleepy bourg of Inguiniel, through the peace of the Morbihan countryside to the banks of the river Scorff and back, passing by a former mill and with an optional extension to another. Farmland alternates with deep woods providing shade for a hot day.

DIRECTIONS

1. Go down *Rue de la Résistance*, opposite the church. After 500m, in Kergal Vras, take the road on the right, which immediately divides. Bear right onto the farm track. Where it divides, bear right ahead. Where the track ends, turn right along the far side of the hedgerow. Follow the edges of the field up to the top corner. Continue ahead into the next field, following the right edge up to the road.

2. Turn left along the road for 300m, over the hill, and take the grassy path on the right. Follow the path down to the bottom, then bear right into the trees. Passing through scrubland, then with a field on the right, the path approaches a wood, swings left and right to enter it.

After 100m, at a multiple cross-roads of paths, turn sharp left into a hollow and on the other side bear right to continue in the same direction as before. On leaving the woods turn left onto a grassy track coming up from the right.

3. In 50m at the cross-roads of tracks, turn left then go straight on past the no-entry sign into the hamlet of Penhoët-St-Lalu. Continue ahead as the track becomes a road. In 50m, at a junction, take the grassy track ahead, bearing right. Follow it downhill for about 600m then, before the bottom, take the path leaving to the right.

Diversion (15 mins): to see Moulin Neuf on the River Scorff, continue on the track downhill, bending left at the bottom and crossing the river at the mill. Return to this point to continue the walk.

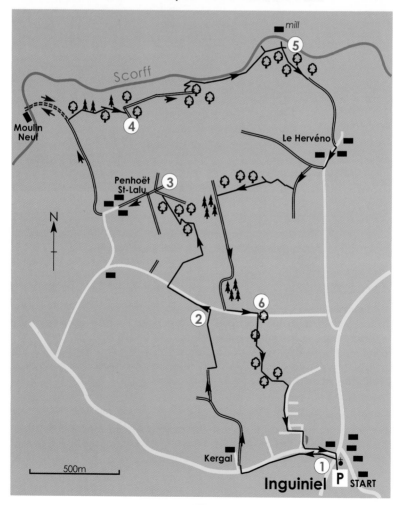

Where the path becomes difficult to trace in a pine wood, walk up to the right behind the first line of trees and soon the path re-appears. On entering the pines again it is just about discernible, more or less straight, going slightly left. Bear right on a larger path arriving from the left.

4. At a wider track, turn sharp left along it, back into the trees and round to the right. After going downhill, just as the track levels out, ignore the track into a field on the left and take the path to the left 20m further on. This zig-zags down to the river.

Continue along the river to the right (upstream), ignoring the path joining from the right. At a three-way intersection of paths, bear right.

5. At the broad, grassy path going uphill away from the river, turn right. The path becomes a track and arrives in the hamlet of Le Hervéno. Here turn right onto the road. After 150m take the track on the right, then shortly afterwards turn left onto another track. Follow this over the hill, then take the track on the right.

At a Y-junction bear left. At the T-junction turn left and follow the track along the edge of the plantation, leaving it at its corner and making for another plantation 400m away.

Here turn right and follow the track around the plantation to the road. Turn left and follow the road for 200m.

6. At a group of chestnut trees on the right, leave the road and walk down the left-hand edge of the field. Follow the path through a clump of trees, then again down the left-hand edge of the field for 50m. Here turn left into the trees, down a bank and up the other side. Follow the main path meandering through the wood, eventually bearing left and reaching a road.

Here turn right, follow the road downhill through a housing estate, turning left at the bottom, where the road bends right, and emerging just above a pond. Go down to the main road and turn left to regain the centre of Inguiniel.

OTHER WALKS in the area:

Inguiniel : *Le tour du bourg* 10kms 3hrs Waymarked yellow. Explores the countryside to the south and east of the town.

WALK 16: Arzon

Length 10kms	Time 3½hrs	Level 2 (but some steps)

Location & parking: *Port de Kerners*, near Arzon. Turn right for Kerners at the first roundabout after the Arzon town sign.
In Kerners, turn left at the junction, then right to *Port de Kerners* – the car-park is at the end of this road.

Refreshments: at Port Navalo, also bar/crêperie by car-park at Kerners.

Arzon lies just inland at the end of the *Presqu'île de Rhys*, which curves around the south of the Gulf of Morbihan. The walk sets out along the less developed coastline north of Arzon, returning through the town via a dolmen or two, and with a possible extension to take a close look at a tide mill. There are spectacular views of the gulf and its islands, including Gavrinis with its neolithic cairn and Er Lannic with its cromlech half on land and half in the water. When the tide is going out the water races towards the narrow mouth of the gulf – it's like watching a bath emptying. Local pre-occupations are oysters and messing about in boats.

DIRECTIONS

1. Walk ahead down the road from the far right corner of the car-park. On reaching the coast, turn left along the coast path.

Around the headland, the island of Hent Tenn comes into view and beyond it the larger Île de la Jument. Further into the next inlet, Gavrinis appears beyond these two, with the smaller island of Er Lannic in front of it. Both the cairn on Gavrinis and the cromlech of Er Lannic can be seen more clearly later on the walk.

2. At the top of the first inlet is a small car-park and just beyond it the path divides: take the right fork to follow the coast path around the headland.

3. Towards the top of the next inlet there is a grassy area with a couple of seats and from here the coast path leaves the shore and follows the road, behind some houses built on the shoreline.

Just before the road bends left, at another grassy seating area take the coast path leaving to the right. At the shore, turn left along the wall, outside the hedge.

At the top of the next point, the **Pointe de Penbert**, the path divides. Go right to get the closest view of Gavrinis and Er Lannic, then return the few paces to this junction and continue on the other path.

Continue round to the next point, regarded as a viewpoint. Indeed from here there is a wider view round to the left, to the town of Locmariaquer on the far shore and, further left, the mouth of the Gulf and out into the Bay of Quiberon.

4. Continuing on towards the next headland, the *Pointe de Bilgroix*, the path leaves the coast again to pass behind a house and its garden and then down a very narrow passage between two high fences, emerging onto a road. Here turn left.

Alternative: if the tide is high, the *Pointe de Bilgroix* can be reached by road from here.

100m up the road, just before a wooden fence, turn right down a narrow passage way. Follow this down to the beach and turn left along it. Follow the beach all the way to the *Pointe de Bilgroix*.

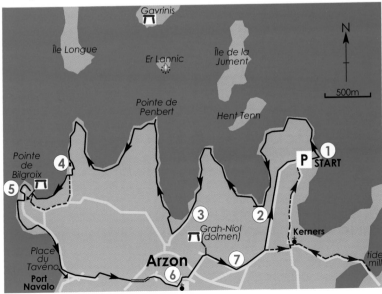

53

Tide mill at Pen Castel

At the point there are some seats, a map of the Gulf, and a large granite statue of Ste-Anne, the patron saint of Brittany.

5. From the far side of the *Pointe de Bilgroix*, follow the road inland for 100m.

Here there is a small cairn on the left with information boards in English as well as French.

Opposite the cairn, follow the coastal path through a gap between the houses, back to the shore. Here turn left along the shore towards Port Navalo.

Soon the path leaves the shore again and joins a road. Bear right on the road and follow it right down to a boulevard along the shore that leads to the *Place du Tavéno* (actually a triangle with a car-park in the middle) at the top of the harbour.

Walk up the left side of the *Place du Tavéno* and on into *Rue Ste-Anne* (no through road), bearing left onto the footpath at the end.

Continue over a road with a zebra crossing, and down the *Chemin des Saules* opposite. At the crossroads continue ahead on the tarmac, still the *Chemin des Saules*, and, arriving in Arzon, go ahead to the church.

6. In front of the church take the road to the left of the bakery, then shortly after take the street on the right, *Rue du Presbytère*. Just past the car-park on the left take the *Rue du Graniol*. Continue ahead at the junction, still on the same road.

Go right at the mini-roundabout on the *Chemin du Saint Sacrement*.

Alternative: continue ahead at the mini-roundabout to see the dolmen (allée couverte) of *Grah-Niol,* on the left in 100m. Return to the mini-roundabout and take the *Chemin du Saint Sacrement*.

7. **At a major road, bear left along it, and continue ahead at the next junction, passing the village sign of Kerners. The next road on the left leads directly to the car-park at *Port de Kerners*.**

Alternative Route (extra 100m): continue to the centre of Kerners and take the road to the left of the church, to emerge into *Place St-Nicolas*. Continue ahead up the village street with old stone cottages on either side. This road eventually arrives at the car-park at *Port de Kerners*.

Optional Extension (2km): take the road to the right of the church in Kerners for 1km, as far as the tide mill at Pen Castel. Return to the church in Kerners.

OTHER WALKS in the area:

Île aux Moines - the largest island in the Gulf of Morbihan with regular boat services from Vannes, Port Navalo, Locmariaquer, Auray, Port Blanc (Baden) and Larmor Baden. There are several marked circuits and there-and-back paths. See the Dolmen and Menhir of Penhap, and the Cromlech of Kergonan. (NB - this island can get a little crowded in summer.)

Île d'Arz - the second largest island in the Gulf, with similar boat services to the Île aux Moines, has a 16km walk around its coast.

Gulf of Morbihan - a continuous coastal footpath runs right around the Gulf from Arzon to Locmariaquer - more than 180kms.

Presqu'Île de Rhuys - the whole peninsula can be explored with the aid of a folder of 16 pull-out maps of circular walks - available from TOs on the peninsula.

PLACES OF INTEREST nearby:

Kerners The 17th century tide mill at **Pen Castel**, 1km from Kerners (see above, point 7, alternative 2).

The **Butte de Caesar**, a large tumulus to the right of the main road into Arzon, just before the turning to Kerners. Open all year.

Cairn du Petit Mont (2.5kms S) a neolithic cairn on a promontory at the mouth of the Port du Crouesty, south of Arzon. Open from end of March to beginning of November.

Château de Suscinio (12kms E, see Walk No.22). Open all year. www.suscinio.info

Gavrinis - the neolithic cairn is highly decorated and well worth a visit. Boat trip from the port of Larmor Baden (SW of Vannes). www.gavrinis.info

WALK 17: Bieuzy-des-Eaux

Length 10kms	Time 2¾hrs	Level 3

Location & parking: Bieuzy-des-Eaux, 15kms SW of Pontivy. Park in car-park by the church.

Refreshments: in Bieuzy and St-Nicolas-des-Eaux, also a bar at Castennec.

From the quiet *bourg* of Bieuzy this route treks across country via tracks and quiet roads to the *Landes de Crano* (pictured), then descends to the valley of the Blavet and returns via the *Site de Castennec* and the *Chapelle St-Gildas*. Views along the way range from charming to the spectacular, and there is plenty of stimulating historical interest.

DIRECTIONS

1. Leave by the road that descends opposite the church tower, but turn right in 50m by the fontaine. Follow this road for 500m and take the track on the right just before the Bieuzy exit sign. Go right where the track divides. Bear left onto a tarmac road through La Motte, and continue on the track when the tarmac ends. Follow the track left, then right and up to the road. Here go left for 500m, down to the main D1.

2. Turn right onto the D1. After 500m take the road on the left, following it right at the houses. At the crossroads go straight over, signed 'Kerhervé'. Where the road turns right, go straight on up the track.

At the top of the hill where the track divides, bear right on a more grassy track. After 100m ignore the track to the right and continue on the footpath ahead.

3. Where the path divides, go right downhill. On entering the trees continue ahead on the main path. After a zig-zag descent, go straight ahead on the grassy path that joins from the right. Arriving at the road, go right along it.

On the left is the railway line, which runs north to south linking St-Brieuc and Auray via Loudeac and Pontivy. This southern section from Pontivy to Auray was completed in December 1864 by the Paris-Orléans railway company, which the previous year had completed its line across southern Brittany as far as Quimper in Finistère. The northern section from Pontivy to St-Brieuc was completed in 1872 by the *Compagnie des Chemins de Fer de l'Ouest*.

Continue on this road, eventually passing under the railway, and alongside the Blavet, opposite St-Nicolas-des-Eaux.

The Blavet is one of Brittany's major rivers. It is canalised from Hennebont as far as Gouarec in Côtes d'Armor. From Pontivy up as far as Gouarec the Blavet provides a section of the Nantes-Brest Canal, though now sadly interrupted by the barrage of *Lac de Guerlédan*.

4. 50m short of the road bridge at St-Nicolas-des-Eaux take the footpath on the right that climbs back up the hillside. At the road,

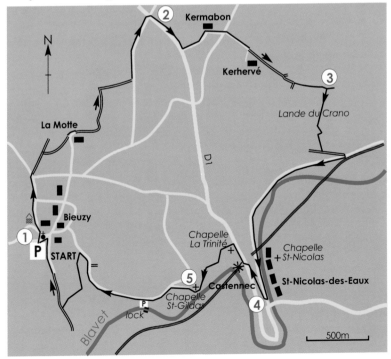

Chapel of St-Gildas

bear right across to the stone-built belvedere, climb the steps and admire the view.

This impressive promontory is the *Site de Castennec* (Castel-Noec). Known as Sulis in Roman times, it was on the main road from Carhaix (Vorgium) to Vannes. Its dominating position, within the territory of the ruling house of Porhoët, led to its use for a feudal fortress. Here was the seat of Alain, brother of Geoffroi de Porhoët, before he settled at Rohan early in the 12th century.

From the belvedere continue up the road. 50m past the *Chapelle de La Trinité* take the footpath on the left. Follow the path ahead between the houses and straight on downhill. On entering the woods bear right down a steep slope, across the stream and up the other side. Continue past large rocks to emerge on the grassy bank of the Blavet.

The Chapel of St-Gildas, dating from 1524, is the only troglodyte chapel in Brittany. It is built at the site where the 6th century St-Gildas and his disciple Bieuzy are said to have established an oratory whilst evangelising Cornouaille. In summer the chapel is often open by virtue of the 'Art in the Chapels' scheme that displays the work of various artists in chapels that might otherwise be little used.

5. Walk to the left of the chapel between two stone pillars (actually canal kilometre markers). **Continue up the road to the T-junction and turn left along the road.** Soon the sound of rushing water announces the presence of a lock and weir on the Blavet.

Continue on the road to the head of a valley. Ignoring the track on the right, follow the road as it bears left, then take the footpath on the left, just before the road bears right and climbs again.

Follow the footpath through the woods on the other side of the valley. At the track, turn sharp right uphill. Soon the church of Bieuzy is visible ahead to guide you back to your starting point.

OTHER WALKS in the area:

Bieuzy There is a longer version of this walk (21kms 5½ hrs). Go straight on at point **3.**, following yellow waymarking, to cross the Blavet canal at Rimaison and return via the chapel of St-Nicodème (well worth seeing) to rejoin this walk at the bridge in St-Nicolas-des-Eaux (**4.**).

Alternatively, start at St-Nicodème and descend to the Blavet, turning left downstream all the way to-St Nicolas-des-Eaux, then follow this walk to the chapel of St-Gildas and back, return across country from the chapel of St-Nicolas in St-Nicolas des Eaux. (See *Central Brittany Coast to Coast*, Walk 9.)

Bubry (9km W) There are several circuits based on Bubry. Ask at the mairie - 02 97 51 70 07

Melrand (3kms W) *Circuit botanique du Guelhouit* 9km 2hrs. Ask at the mairie - 02 97 39 54 61

PLACES OF INTEREST nearby:

St-Nicolas-des-Eaux The *Chapelle de St-Nicolas* has carved and painted beams dated 1534. Waterfront with cafés, restaurants etc. River trips possible, or hire a boat.

Melrand (10km N) *Village de l'An Mil* A museum based on a reconstruction of a Breton village in the year 1000AD.
02 97 39 57 89 Open May to August.

WALK 18: Callac

Length 9kms	**Time** 2½hrs	**Level** 2 (optional 3)

Location & parking: From Sérent, take the D776 direction Vannes for 1km, then turn right onto the D133 to Callac. Here turn right by the church and follow the road out to the Grotto (on the left). Park at the fork beyond the Grotto.

Refreshments: none on route.

Station of the Cross

Callac is a small *bourg* within the commune of Plumelec. Deep in the Morbihan countryside, religious observance is still strong and one has a definite sense of this at the start of the walk. Essentially a rural ramble, it takes in a charming isolated chapel and has an optional extension to see a historic château dating from the 14th century.

In the mid 20th century, Callac had an exceptional priest, le Père Binard. He and his parishioners turned a disused slate quarry into a testament of their faith, comprising a grotto and the 14 stations of the cross, depicted in life-size sculptures. Perhaps the most extraordinary element of the site is the Chapel of St-Joseph, a 16th century chapel which was removed stone by stone from Le Mont at Guéhenno (10kms to the north west) and rebuilt here at Callac. It is lovingly cared for by local people and opened every day, weather permitting. Le Père Binard is buried here.

DIRECTIONS
1. **From the car-park return to the grotto and take the path climbing just to its left. This steep, stepped path, follows the stations of the cross, then leads down steps toward the Chapel of St-Joseph, visible through the trees.**

Alternative: to avoid the steep climb around the stations of the cross, there is a less arduous path to the chapel via the road on the right past the Grotto.

Continue past the chapel to the road and turn right.

In La Ville Hervé, ignore the road to the left. Continue to where the road bends left, and take the track on the right.

At the wood in 200m, take the track on the left. At the bottom, bear right through the village and take the road on the left just before the T-junction. After 50m turn left again down a track and continue ahead.

2. After 350m the path turns right and appears to end; here turn left between two fields to meet a track again at the opposite hedgerow.

At a T-junction with a small road, turn right and left again immediately onto another grassy track.

Where this meets another track, bear right and continue down through the farm, then on the road that leads down to the D133.

Turn left and follow the D133 up to the outskirts of Callac.

3. At the top of the hill, where the road bends left into Callac, turn right onto a track. Follow this across open farmland, down to the village of Pont de Jonc.

Here turn left to pass between houses and onto a tarmac road. Where it turns left to leave the village, go straight ahead on a track.

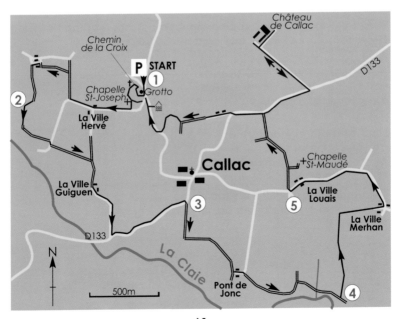

61

This pleasant track through the woods soon has a steep drop on the right, down to the river Claie.

50m after the track bends left, take the track on the right, following it down to the bottom and up the other side.

4. At the top, take the path sharp left. Eventually it leaves the woods and, in the middle of open ground, turns right towards La Ville Merhan. Here turn left at the crossroads. Follow the road for 700m, through La Ville Louais.

5. Opposite a road on the left, take the track on the right. The chapel of St-Maudé is visible on the right; turn right to visit it but return to this track to continue the walk.

The Chapelle St-Maudé was saved from ruin by a team of volunteers. It still carries the arms of the Callac family, on a vast stone escutcheon to the right of the south door.

Continue on the track up to the road and turn left along it.

Alternative: turn right on the road and take the first road on the left to visit the *Château de Callac* (1km). Having looked at the *château* from the outside only – it is private – return to this point.

At the far side of the *château*, facing northeast, are the original round towers of the 15th century *château fort*. The rest is 17th and 18th century. During the Revolution it was a hiding place for refractory priests and a centre of the Chouan movement of counter-revolutionaries and royalists. This spirit of resistance was revived in WW2 when the château became the headquarters of Free French parachutists in June 1944.

Where the road bends left, bear right on a minor road and passing a few houses continue ahead on a grassy track.

At a T-junction of tracks, turn right, away from the *bourg*. Follow this track down to the road. Here turn right.

Detour: to the right of the road, a stepped path climbs to the 16th century *Fontaine La Touche Berthelot*, which came originally from St-Malo Des Trois Fontaines.

Follow the road downhill to regain the Grotto and your starting point.

OTHER WALKS in the area:

Plumelec (8km NW) The *mairie* has details of other walks in the commune of Plumelec, ranging from 5 - 18kms. 02 97 42 24 27 - mairie@plumelec.com www.plumelec.com

WALK 19: Elven

Length 10kms	Time 3hrs	Level 2

Location & parking: Elven, just off the N166, 13kms NE of Vannes. Drive through the parking in front of the church to find Rue Coëdelo, which has its own car-park, half way down on the right.

Refreshments: in Elven, none on route.

The main attraction of Elven is the Château de Largoët, sometimes called *La Forteresse de L'Argoët* (the fortress of the forest). It is noted for having the highest *donjon* or keep in France at either 45m or 57m, depending from where it is measured. The *château* is private but is open to the public every day during high season. Only the gatehouse is visible from this walk, which skirts the grounds and visits the nearby *Manoir de Kerleau.*

DIRECTIONS

1. From the car-park turn right and take the first road on the left. At the lavoir, turn right onto a woodland path (can be muddy after wet weather). After 600m the path crosses a steam. Shortly afterwards, where it divides, go right up a *chemin creux*. Passing a granite cross on the left and by-passing Kerbody on the right, the path eventually bends right, then left to meet another path coming up from the right. Here, go left along it.

2. Bear right by a tin barn to meet a little tarmac road. Follow this to a T-junction and turn right.

The distant view to the right from here is of the Landes de Lanvaux, a ridge of heathland stretching from Baud in the west almost as far as Redon in the east. It is a wild, uncultivated area, a refuge of Chouans in the aftermath of the Revolution.

At the next junction in 100m, turn left (signed to Kerleau).100m after the road bends left, look for the Manoir de Kerleau on the right.

The Manoir de Kerleau dates from the 15th century. In the 17th century it was owned by the Descartes family. René Descartes, the famous philosopher (1596-1650 - 'I think, therefore I am') visited Kerleau c.1625 to be godfather to a nephew.

Continue past the large (disused) manor farm complex. Where an avenue of trees crosses the road at an angle, bear left down the avenue.

3. At the end, pass between crumbling stone pillars and turn right along the road. Follow the road for 1.6kms to a T-junction. Here turn left and after a further 650m, opposite the first road arriving from the right, take the footpath on the left. Follow this path through the trees, then ahead on a track across open ground to the road.

Detour: At the road, turn left to the gatehouse of the Château de Largoët. Return to where the track crosses the road.

The gatehouse has a large stone carving of a hare at each corner of the roof, recalling the favourite pastime, hunting hares, of a former owner, le Maréchal de Rieux..

4. Cross the road and follow the track along the left hand edge of the field, at the corner of which bear left then right into the trees. The path then passes some new houses on the right and ends at the housing estate road. Here turn left along a track, away from the houses. Opposite a water metering station on the left, take the farm track on the right, going between fields. The track eventually arrives at a road in the village of Kerandou. Here turn right and follow the road up to the main road, turning left to walk back into Elven. Look for the church tower to locate the car-park.

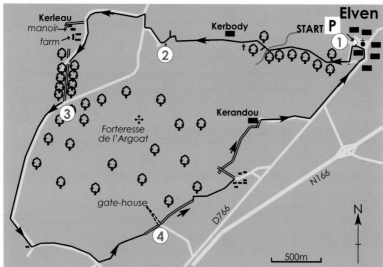

PLACES OF INTEREST nearby:

Château de Largoët, Open 15th March - 2nd Nov - every day in high season, otherwise various days and times. Tel. 02 97 53 35 96
Vannes (15kms SW via N166) the old city, walls and fortifications, cathedral, medieval streets and the port are all worth visiting.

WALK 20: Langonnet

Length 10½kms	Time 3hrs	Level 2

Location & parking: *l'Etang de Langonnet*. From the centre of Langonnet take the D128 towards *Abbaye de Langonnet*. In 1km at Pontigou turn left to La Trinité Langonnet. After 200m turn left to the *Etang de Langonnet* and park near the lake.

Refreshments: none on route. Nearest town is Langonnet.

Leaving the slightly artificial surroundings of the *Etang de Langonnet*, this circuit wanders across rolling countryside to a former Cistercian Abbey, now a missionary centre and retirement home for former missionaries in Africa. The resulting museum of African artefacts is not to be missed, when open. On the way out the walk passes a Bronze Age tumulus and a feudal motte, and on the way back a 16th century chapel and an unusual calvaire.

DIRECTIONS

1. **From the parking at the end of the lake, walk to the right and, leaving the lake, go down the wide grassy way between the trees. Turn left at the bank, onto another wide grassy way and after 150m turn right over a little bridge and up to a stony track. Bear right along the track, which becomes a road through the village of Restemblei Len, swinging right to join a larger road. Cross over this and go up the road to the left on the other side, signed to Restemblei d'en Haut. Where it turns left at the top, go straight on, along a straight stony track. Follow this for almost 1km to a T-junction of tracks.**

2. Here turn right and then note the tumulus hidden in the trees on the left.

Tumuli are normally from the Bronze Age (3000-1500BC) and this one is no exception. Inside would be a burial chamber. Most have been either robbed or excavated at some time since the beginning of the 19th century and this tumulus shows evidence of some such disturbance near its summit. It was listed as a historic monument in 1946.

Turn left immediately past the tumulus and continue for 500m towards the village of Kermain. Look out for the feudal motte to the right of the track, hidden by trees.

This is the site of a small castle, which may well have been a simple wooden construction originally, the seat of a local lord who had the right of high justice. The 'seigneurie' was held by the Kermain family in 1426 but by 1448 it had passed to others. The successor to the motte is the *Manoir de Kermain*, a 16th/17th century manor house set back from the road about 200m away. It was common for the old home to be re-used in some way and this one had a dovecote built upon it. Some stonework remains on the summit and one can speculate how much of it is the dovecote and how much from some earlier building.

Continuing past the motte go straight on where the track joins a road. (Entrance to the manoir on the right.) Continue on this road past some fenced enclosures, a former zoo.

At the junction, go straight on and down the road as far as the river but do not cross over. (The buildings ahead on the opposite hill are a technical college.)

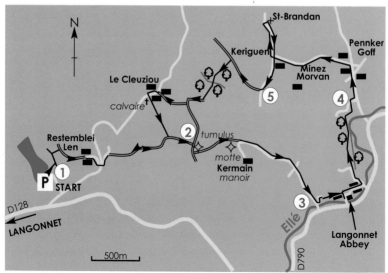

3. Before the bridge turn sharp left and climb steeply up the road. The end of the road is a private driveway but just in front of the gates, on the right, is a gap in the wall that leads into the grounds of the abbey, by a statue of Our Lady. Walk down the avenue and between stone pillars out onto the abbey car-park with a building on the right.

To visit the Abbey turn right at the end of this building and cross to the entrance to the cloisters opposite. The African Museum is in the building you first passed.

Originally a Cistercian abbey, founded in 1136 on land granted by Conan III Duke of Brittany, Langonnet Abbey has had a chequered history. After the revolution it become a national haras, breeding war horses. The haras moved to Hennebont when the abbey was taken over by the *Congregation du Saint-Esprit*, a missionary organisation who are still there today. Visitors are welcome.

From the abbey car-park continue in the same direction as you arrived, between two long buildings. Through the stone pillared gateway at the far end, turn immediately sharp left and follow the road up and away from the buildings. Where the road bends left take the path on the right along the edge of the wood. Follow this path through the woods, eventually coming to the river where a broad channel leaves it to take water back to the abbey's mill.

4. At a stony road, turn right, then left onto the tarmac road. Walk up the hill to Penkergoff. In Penkergoff turn second left to Minez Morvan and Keriguen.

The hill of Minez (Menez) Morvan is thought to be the final fortified position of the early 9th century Breton leader Morvan in his ill-fated defiance of Louis the Pious of France.

At the T-junction in Keriguen, turn right for 200m to the chapel of St-Brandan.

Return to the junction in Keriguen and continue straight on over the hill. (At the top of the hill on the curve of a road junction on the left are four standing stones that look like the remains of a cromlech, or stone circle.)

5. After a few hundred metres, where the road bends left, take the track on the right. After 500m look for the *chemin creux* on the left. Follow the *chemin creux* and continue on a path across marshy land through the woods. The path is raised on a bank for most of the way but there is a point half way where a stream crosses that could be difficult in wet weather.

The path emerges at the end of a straight track. Follow this to the right, round a left hand bend, then take the track on the right.

At the top of the rise the track enters the village of Le Cleuziou. Turn left onto the road as far as the calvaire on the left, just past another

track on the left. Leaving the calvaire, return to the track immediately by it and follow it over the hill and on to a T-junction of tracks. Here turn right and retrace the outward route to return to Restemblei Len and the lake.

OTHER WALKS in the area:

Langonnet: the mairie (02 97 23 96 34) has leaflets for several walks in the area from 4 to 13kms starting from Langonnet and from La Trinité Langonnet (9kms N).

PLACES OF INTEREST nearby:

Langonnet - the church dates from the end of the 11th century and is a combination of the Roman and Gothic styles of architecture.

La Trinité Langonnet (approx 8km NNW of Langonnet) - interesting church and an elaborate fontaine a short walk away.

Le Faouët (10km S) - 17th century market hall.

WALK 21: Noyal-Muzillac

Length 10kms	Time 3hrs	Level 3

Location & parking: Noyal-Muzillac on the D5 between Muzillac and Questembert. Park in front of the *mairie*.

Refreshments: in Noyal-Muzillac, none on route.

Noyal-Muzillac is one of those little towns noted for its interesting and characteristic architecture - including 17th and 18th century houses with pigeon-holes below the eaves. The country to the west is also very beautiful with rolling hills, wooded valleys and babbling brooks. There are quite a few mills in the area, one of them on this walk. The walk starts with a *sentier botanique*, its information panels not only identifying the trees and bushes but giving a snippet of tree-lore for each - did you know, for example, that the ash tree could be useful in the treatment of snake bites?

DIRECTIONS

1. **Facing away from the mairie, go past the pharmacy and bear left. Turn right immediately towards the 'Complex Sportif'. Walk down through its car-park and bear left then right to take a broad footpath under the trees.**

At the road turn right and left again immediately on a footpath descending into the woods. Go to the right of the lake. You are now following a *Sentier Botanique*. **Across the bridge and up the other side, bear right on a path signed 'La Gravelle 400m'. The path descends to run alongside the stream on the right. La Gravelle is a rock on the left hand side of the path.**

The legend of the rock is that Gargantua, during one of his visits to Breton soil, had one foot on the church spire of Ambon and wanted to put his other foot on the spire of Noyal Muzillac, but being bothered by a stone in his shoe, he dropped it here, leaving this delightful memento of his visit.

Continue past La Gravelle.

2. Pass through a wooden barrier and turn right (the end of the Sentier Botanique) then right again at another barrier. On reaching a track, follow it uphill to the left (ignore the track ahead). Follow it round to the right along the top of the field, then left into the next field and round to the right.

Where the track goes left, down towards the farm, leave it, bearing right along the top of the field then bearing right again through the field boundary to bear left on a track.

3. Ignore a track joining from the right but take the next on the right

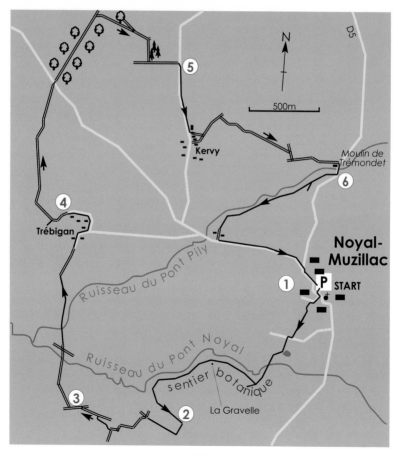

50m later, signed 'Trébigan 1300m'. Follow this track down over a stream (*Ruisseau du Pont Noyal*) by a little stone bridge (*Le Pont Madame*). Continue ahead, crossing a raised track, to a wooden bridge over another stream. Continue up the other side into the village of Trébigan. Here follow the road round to the right and bear left at the Y-junction.

4. Continue on this road until it ends, then ahead on the track. Where a footpath forks left downhill, bear right on the track. At the road, go straight over onto a track through the wood.

Where a field appears to the left, take the track on the right, uphill (ignore the yellow cross on a tree). At the top, continue ahead on a track arriving from the left. At the plantation, bear right along its edge, turning left at the far end and continue to the road.

5. At the road go right (signed Kervy 450m). In Kervy, just past a stone house with a slate-covered gable, turn left down the track. At a T-junction in 50m turn left and follow this broad, well-worn track, ignoring others to right and left, all the way to the D5. Here turn right and go over the bridge by an old mill.

The *Moulin de Trémandet*, besides the normal work of milling grain into flour, was also used to process hemp.

6. A few metres past the bridge take the footpath on the right (signed Pont Pily). Where the path divides bear right ahead to follow the valley. At the end, the path reaches some houses and comes to a road. Turn left up the road and follow it straight into Noyal-Muzillac.

PLACES OF INTEREST nearby:

Muzillac (5.5kms S) *Moulin de Pen Mur*. The mill dates from the 15th century, when it was owned by Francois II, last duke of Brittany. It was converted to a paper mill in the 1940s, later to a book-binding enterprise, then abandoned. Rescued in 1986, it now makes paper using traditional 18th century methods. Open Apr-Sept every day (closed Sun am until end of June), Oct-Mar weekends and holidays. 02 97 41 43 79 www.moulin-pen-mur.com

Le Guerno (5kms E) *Parc Animalier et Botanique de Branféré* Almost 1,000 animals of over 120 species cohabit freely in a park of 40 hectares. Open Feb to Nov. 02 97 42 94 66 www.branfere.com

WALK 22: Suscinio

Length 10kms	Time 2½hrs	Level 2

Location & parking: Château de Suscinio, signed from the D780 near Sarzeau, Presqu'île de Rhuys. Park in the château visitors' car-park.

Refreshments: crêperie/bar near the car-park at Suscinio. None on route.

It would be a shame to come here for this walk and not allow enough time to visit the 13th century château as well. Favourite residence of the Dukes of Brittany for two centuries, it was bought as a ruin by the department of Morbihan in 1965 and has since been restored. Today it houses an impressive collection of medieval floor tiles. The surrounding land is flat, mostly marshes, some of which have in the past been exploited for salt. The forest of Suscinio is said to have extended into an area now covered by the sea. The Bay of Suscinio is also a contender for the site of King Gradlon's lost city of Ys. The walk starts from the château, explores the country to the west, now farmed, but once a ducal hunting park, and returns along the coast.

DIRECTIONS

1. **From the car-park, walk to the left of the château and on into the village of Suscinio. Continue ahead past a no-entry sign and follow the road sharp right around the last gable of the Moulin Vert.**

72

Le Moulin Vert is a medical institution, here housed in a converted 19th century barracks for customs officers.

Follow the road for 1.5kms, then bear left at the oblique T-junction. Just before the first house on the right, turn right onto a green lane. Follow this for 1.5km to Kergorange.

To the left of the green lane is a stone wall marking the limit of the ducal park of Glisgoët. To the right is a marsh, the *Étang de Calzac*.

2. In Kergorange turn left at the T-junction (care needed – this road can be busy). At the top of the hill, take the left fork, signed to Lan Hoëdic. Continue on the road, through La Noëdic.

(Note the two differnt name styles, one Breton, the other a garbled French version.)

3. Where the road bends right, continue ahead on a footpath, signed *Chemin pietonnier plage*.

Follow this path to the shore, turning left along the coastal path that runs just behind the beach.

4. On reaching a point, with a stone walled enclosure, take the easier path to the left of it.

The old path round the seaward side has been seriously eroded and though still passable it is quite tricky. Here is Beg Lann, a 18th/19th century fort and customs post. It was sold in 1865 to *Les Pères de Picpus*, a missionary organisation, who still use it as a retreat.

Continue ahead through the wooden barrier. Bear right through a car-park and along behind the sea wall.

Disused salt marshes lie to the left.

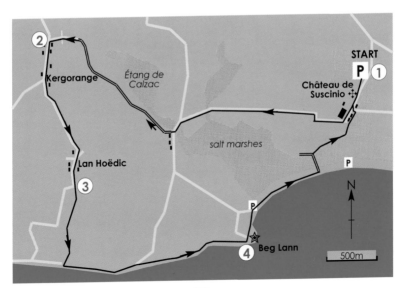

Shortly before another car-park, take the green lane on the left and follow it through the marshes. Where it bends left, take the path to the right. At the road, bear left then right to regain the château and its car-park.

OTHER WALKS in the area:

Presqu'Île de Rhuys The whole peninsula can be explored with a folder of 16 pull-out maps of circular walks - available from TOs at St-Colombier, Sarzeau and Port du Crouesty.

PLACES OF INTEREST nearby:

Suscinio - *Château de Suscinio:* open all year, every day except Dec 24/25, hours vary according to season. www.suscinio.info

St-Armel - *Les Marais de Lasné:* salt marshes restored to working order and producing salt; also a nature reserve. Guided visits - TO St-Colombier, Sarzeau. 02 97 26 45 26

St-Gildas-de-Rhuys - the 11th century abbey church of St-Gildas, celebrates its thousandth year in 2008.

WALK 23: Trégréhen

Length 10kms	Time 2½hrs	Level 3

Location & parking: 3km south east of Muzillac. D5 southwards from Muzillac (direction Billiers), under the N165 and turn left onto C301 (signed to Arzal). After 1.5kms turn left, signed to Trégréhenne. Turn left in the village and park near the chapel.

Refreshments: none on route.

There used to be an abbey at Billiers, *Abbaye Notre-Dame de Prières*, founded in 1252 and flourishing until the Revolution. The monks and abbot were expelled 1792. Nothing remains of the abbey buildings but a chapel rebuilt in 1841, but still housing the

tomb of Duc Jean I, the abbey's founder. Two of the abbey's boundary markers (*bornes*) are passed on this walk on the way down to the Vilaine. These hillsides were covered by vineyards until the 20th century, when the ceps were killed off by phylloxera. Originally belonging to the abbey, they were latterly owned in small parcels by local people who cultivated them for their own consumption. The river Vilaine is here at its estuary, bordered by oyster beds and constantly changing its appearance with the tides.

DIRECTIONS

1. **From the chapel walk up the road (southwards, past the road you drove in on) turn right at the fork, signed La Lande Verrien.**

2. **After 800m, where a track crosses the road, take a few paces down the track on the left to find a *borne de prière*, by a field entrance on the right.**

Four *bornes de prière* mark the boundary of the lands and vineyards belonging to the Cistercian abbey at Billiers. The *bornes* are carved with a lozenge and an ermine.

Where the road becomes a track, continue ahead for 1.2km, ignoring the left fork after 250m and any other tracks to the right or left.

At the road bear left along it for 200m, then turn right at the junction. There is another *borne de prière* on the right.

3. Bear right with the road, then first left between two rows of buildings, continuing on the footpath ahead. Follow this footpath over the hill and down the other side towards the River Vilaine. It was on these south-facing slopes that vines were cultivated.

At the road turn left along it. On the banks of the Vilaine, turn right along the coastal path.

4. After 2km, at a cove, bear left along a track arriving from the right. Continue past the house on the opposite side of the cove and turn right on a footpath going inland. Continue up the left side of a field, then right downhill between the fields. At the bottom, turn left along the bottom edge of the field and continue ahead onto the track.

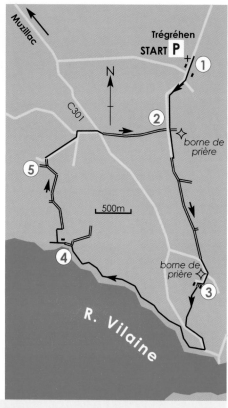

5. At a junction of tracks, bear right up to the road, then right along it. At the triangular road junction, bear left, then in 50m at the T-junction go right. At the junction with the C301, go straight on up the track.

Follow the main track ahead to the road at Point 2. Here turn left back to Trégréhen.

PLACES OF INTEREST nearby:

Billiers *Dolmen du Crapaud*, on the coast path just west of this walk, south of Billiers. Named the 'dolmen of the toad' because of its shape.

WALK 24: Lac de Guerlédan

Length 11kms	Time 3¼hrs	Level 3/4

Location & parking: St-Aignan. From Mur-de-Bretagne take the D18, direction Cléguérec, and turn right immediately after crossing the canal. Park behind the church on the right.

Refreshments: none on route. Bar/restaurant in St-Aignan, as well as a crêperie nearby.

The construction of this lake and its towering barrage for a hydro-electric station in the 1920s effectively cut the Nantes-Brest canal in half. Through-navigation across Brittany was no longer possible as the cost of including a ladder of locks for barges was

prohibitive. 12 kilometres of the Blavet valley were flooded, engulfing 400 hectares of woodland, houses, locks and lockhouses from the original canal. When the lake is drained for maintenance every ten years, the ghostly spectre of this lost canal reappears.

DIRECTIONS

1. From the car-park turn right on the road and go straight on at the junction. After 100m take the road on the right opposite the tennis court. Bear left at the house and continue ahead on the track. Ignore the track to the right that passes over the bridge (unless you want to look at the remnants of the Nantes-Brest Canal). When level with the electricity plant on the opposite bank, take the second path climbing to the left. Follow it up the steep hillside, bearing right, and turn left on reaching the little road.

2. At the roundabout/car-park, take the path that leaves uphill from the far right corner, by the notice board. Follow this path for 700m to the Chapel of Ste-Tréphine.

The chapel is built on the site of a dark age fortification, Castel Finans, thought to have been one of the strongholds of the 6th century Breton chief Conomor. "In legend, Conomor, a sadistically cruel man, was supposed to have murdered many members of his family, most famously his young second wife Tréphine, daughter of the Count of Vannes. He cut off the head of this unfortunate girl when she became pregnant, because of a prophecy that he would be killed by his own son. St-Gildas performed a miracle to restore her body to life, although Conomor still succeeded in beheading her infant son, Trémeur, years later." (Discovering the History of Brittany - Wendy Mewes)

Continue ahead from the chapel on the wide grassy track, going straight on at two consecutive junctions. After several hundred metres, the track bends left uphill and goes through a barrier to a *fontaine* and *lavoir* on the left. Continue a few metres to a clearing where several tracks meet.

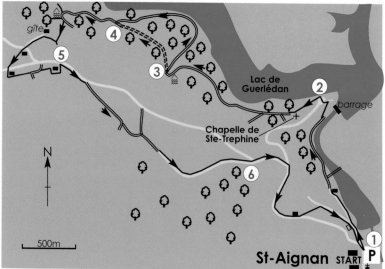

78

3. Here, take the track on the right going downhill.

Alternative: to avoid a descent to the lake shore and the long climb back again, take the second track on the right (uphill) and resume the directions from point 4.

At the lakeside this track is briefly joined by the GR341S that follows the shore. Stay on the broad track as it bends left to climb back up the hill.

4. At a T-junction of tracks turn right. Stay on the main track, round a left hand bend with a track joining from the right, past a fontaine on the right, past another track joining from the right and take the track signed 'gîte Gros Chêne Botponal'. This track soon narrows to a footpath. At a T-junction, turn right. The gîte soon appears on the right: continue ahead along the road away from the gîte.

At a T-junction, cross over and take the footpath to the right of the driveway. At another road cross straight over to take the footpath to the right of the house. Bear left behind the house and continue through to a track, going straight on along it.

Where the track bends left, continue ahead on a footpath. At the house, bear right down the side of the garden, then left across it and back up the other side to join the driveway, following this up to the road.

5. Here turn right. After 200m, fork right onto a track by a no-entry sign. Where this track turns right after 300m, go ahead on another track. Bear right at a track joining from the left. The track shortly becomes a road: follow it for almost a kilometre.

6. Where another road joins from the left, continue straight ahead. At the next road junction, go right downhill, following the road around a long left hand bend. Just past a house on the left, take the straight path forking left down through the trees. At the road go right to find the tennis court, on the right, that was passed on the outward route. Follow the road back into St-Aignan.

OTHER WALKS in the area:

Lac de Guerlédan A recently completed footpath goes all around the lake, following the shore as closely as is practicable. The northern and southern routes meet in the east at the bridge below the barrage (passed on this walk) and in the west at the lock at Bellvue, the first lock up the Nantes-Brest Canal after Lac de Guerlédan.

PLACES OF INTEREST nearby:

St-Aignan *Museum of Electricity*. Open mid June to mid Sept. Guided visits all year by arrangement.
www.saint-aignan56.fr/musee.htm

WALK 25: Pont-Scorff

Length 11kms	Time 3½hrs	Level 2

Location & parking: Pont-Scorff. Park in the tree-lined *Place de la Maison des Princes,* in front of the *mairie.*

Refreshments: in Pont-Scorff. None on route.

Manoir de St-Urchaud

Pont-Scorff is renowned for its arts and crafts. The streets are lined with workshops and galleries where you can see the artists at work and purchase their creations. In the first part of this walk you are also quite likely to find some works of art literally hanging about in the countryside around the *Manoir de St-Urchaud.* Parts of the *manoir* and its nearby farm are also used as a gallery. The route leaves the town down the river Scorff, crosses in front of Pont-Scorff Zoo, and follows the remote and wild valley of the river Scave before returning over the hills and along the line of a former railway back to Pont-Scorff. There are several opportunities for short-cuts if required but it would be a shame to miss the Scave.

The *Maison des Princes* is a splendid 17th century dwelling of typically Breton architecture. At one time it was used as a law court and thus it has cells. It has housed the *mairie* since 1924 and has been listed as a Historic Monument since the 1930s.

DIRECTIONS

1. From the *mairie* go to the opposite end of the square and down the steps. Turn right at the road. Before the bridge, take the alley 'Chemin du Ronce' on the right. Follow this through to the river bank

and continue alongside the river. Once past the factory on the right, the path leaves the river and rises to join a larger path coming from the right. Follow this for 200m then leave it on a smaller path descending towards the river again.

Leaving the river, the path goes between stone walls with landscaped grounds on the right and comes out just inside a pillared gateway. Go through the gateway and down to the large building, *Manoir St-Urchaud*, on the right hand side of the path. Go past the left end of the building and along the front facing the river.

The *Manoir St-Urchaud* was built about 1650, apparently by the master carpenter Jean Grasset, who went on to build a ship for the king's navy just upstream from here at the 'Saint-Trichaut' slipway. The ground floor appears to have served him as a warehouse, having five doors and no fireplaces. In the 18th century a floor was added, as well as the coachhouse and barn to the left. The large square pavilion was added in the 19th century.

Turn right round the end of the house, then, before the end of the avenue of oaks, turn left on a path that runs alongside the orchard. Go over the wooden bridge and then right where the path divides. At the farm buildings, go straight on up the road.

On reaching the trees, take the forest track on the left. After 200m at a T-junction of paths, turn right uphill. Ignoring the path to the right, continue to the look-out point on the left.

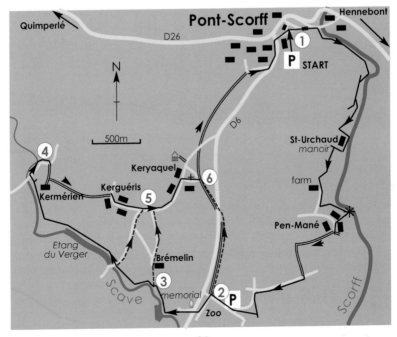

This is known as *Le Rocher du Corbeau* (crow's rock). From here there is a pleasant view over the river, though a little obscured by trees.

Return to the path, which hairpins up to the road, and turn left through the village of Pen-Mané. At the end, turn right along a farm road and follow it for 600m, around a left hand bend to the road.

Here turn right, continue to a T-junction and turn left.

After 50m bear left on a path. A little short of the bottom, take the path on the right and follow it to the road again. Here go left for 20m, right at the T-junction and continue past the entrance to Pont-Scorff Zoo on the left. Take the road on the left, immediately before the T-junction with the D6.

2. Alternative short cut back to Pont-Scorff: turn right opposite the Zoo entrance, across the car-park and go on up the track parallel with the D6. Follow this former railway, crossing over the D6, as far as point 6. and pick up the directions from there.

150m later, a gap in the bank on the right leads to the D6, opposite a war memorial.

In August 1944 the Germans in Lorient, an important U-boat base, did not surrender. They were merely contained by the liberating American and Free French Forces until the final surrender in May 1945.

Take the minor road to the left of the war memorial and continue on a footpath when the road turns right into a driveway. At the water, bear right on the footpath, which follows the valley of the river Scave. After a while, the path leaves the river and comes down to a stony road.

3. Alternative short cut: turn right here to reach point 5. via the village of Brémelin.

Turn left downhill, round the right hand bend and down to the river. Continue along the river (*not* over the bridge) to a road.

Alternative short cut: turn right up the road to reach point 5.

Cross straight over and continue on the path, which runs parallel with and above a narrow lake, *Etang du Verger*.

At the road turn right and walk round the right hand bend.

4. Take the road on the right signed Kermérien. Just before the houses turn left on a track. Follow it over the hill to another farm and village. At the road, turn right and continue round to the left.

5. First one road, then another join from the right (alternative short cuts rejoining). In Keryakel, turn right to the chapel of St-Gildas, and continue past it.

6. Round the left hand bend, leave the road and bear left along the track, an old railway line.

A narrow gauge railway constructed in 1902 by the *Chemins de Fer du Morbihan* linked Lorient with Plouay and was the company's first line. Later their network was extended throughout the department but with the steadily improving road system it became less viable and all their lines were closed by 1947.

Follow the old railway across a road and on into Pont-Scorff. On the outskirts of the town continue to follow the line of the old railway and where the track becomes a road, follow it round to the right and up to the D6, turning left along it. Over the brow of the hill, pass to the right of the Tourist Office, either through the courtyard of the *Cour des Métiers d'Art* or down the 'no entry' street to the right. Arriving in the *Rue Prince de Polignac*, turn right to regain the starting point.

OTHER WALKS in the area:

Cléguer (3.5kms N) Several walks of varying lengths are based on the *bourg*. The commune of Cléguer includes Le Bas Pont-Scorff, across the river bridge from Pont-Scorff itself.

PLACES OF INTEREST nearby:

Pont-Scorff: *L'Odysseum* (near the bridge over the Scorff) Museum of the wild salmon. 02 97 32 42 00

La Maison du Scorff, Le Bas Pont-Scorff (across the Pont Romain, the old bridge over the river)- everything you want to know about the river and its valley.

La Cour des Métiers d'Art, 8 Rue Prince de Polignac, Pont-Scorff. Art gallery and craft workshops.

Zoo de Pont-Scorff (on the D6 toward Lorient) 02 97 32 60 86 Open all year.

WALK 26: St-Jean and the Giant's Tomb

Length 11kms	Time 3hrs	Level 3

Location & parking: parking for Le Tombeau du Géant. Turn left off the D312, 5kms north from Campénéac, and continue ahead to the end of the road, where there is a car-park.

Refreshments: none.

Variety is the keynote of this walk, its points of interest ranging from the stone age, through Arthurian legend, to one of the best preserved *châteaux* in Brittany. The landscape too ranges from high *landes* to deep valleys and, although there is shade much of the way, there are some exposed stretches.

DIRECTIONS

1. **Walk to the end of the car-park and past the no-entry sign. After 200m, turn right with the track. In a further 150m take the footpath to the left.**

Diversion: to see the dolmen called the 'Hôtié de Viviane' continue on the track to its end, then bear left on the footpath, continuing just beyond the rocky summit. Then return to this junction.

This area is on the edge of the Forest of Broceliande, a land of Arthurian legend, hence a neolithic tomb is called the house of Vivianne, the fairy who was born in the *Château de Comper* and became Merlin's pupil. She found the infant Lancelot and raised him. Merlin fell in love with her and built her a *château* under the lake at Comper, from which she became known as the lady of the lake.

84

Keep to the well-worn path as it descends into the valley, following a stream. At some points the path divides, but only temporarily.

2. Where another stream arrives down a valley from the right, turn right and go up that valley.

After the two streams join they continue down into the Valley of No Return, where Morgane, Arthur's half-sister, was in the habit of trapping all unfaithful lovers.

On reaching a T-junction of paths, go right. Where the path broadens to a track, continue ahead, ignoring the track arriving from the left. Follow the track round to the right, ignoring another coming in from the left. At the road, a T-junction by a cross, turn right along the road.

3. At the next T-junction, turn left, then after 100m bear right onto a grassy, rocky path, following it into the trees.

At the road, turn left. After 100m turn right down another path. Where this path reaches a rocky clearing and divides, go right.

At the main road, go right for 200m, then turn right by the pedestrian warning sign. Immediately the Chapel of St-Jean is visible ahead across the old road. To reach the chapel turn left on the old road then right following the sign.

The 17th century Chapel of St-Jean was built on the site of a 6th century hermitage. It belonged to a priory dependent upon the Abbey of Montfort, but later came into the

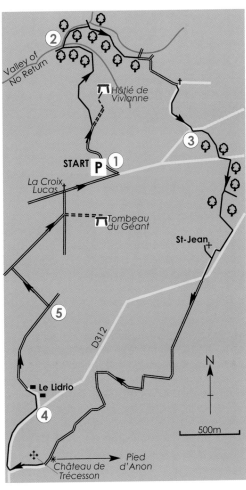

possession of the lords of Trécesson. In 1796 it was the property of Nicolas Bourelle de Sivry (1756-1808), owner of the *Château de Trécesson*; he is buried in the chapel.

Return to take up the old road again, cross over the new road and continue ahead down the long, straight track.

The land to the left is a military training area and firing range, part of the military camp of Coëtquidan, which just after WW2 became the home of the *École Militaire de St-Cyr*, the French equivalent of Sandhurst.

Keep to the track as it zig-zags down the hill.

On nearing the bottom of the hill, look to the left. In the distance is a barren hill with a large regularly shaped rock outcrop, known as the *Pied d'Anon* (literally, the young ass's foot). There is a story that an owner of Trécesson in the early 18th century, having lost everything at the gambling tables of Versailles, staked this rock as a last resort, calling it the '*Manoir du Pied d'Anon*'; from then on he won back all that he had lost.

As the track bends right at the bottom there is a massive dovecote in the corner of a field on the left, but on the right is the *Château de Trécesson*.

Accounts vary of the early history of the *château* but it seems a de Trécesson family existed in the 13th century. In c.1440 a de Trécesson heiress married Duc Jean V's treasurer and guardian of the wardrobe, Eon de Carné. He took the name de Trécesson and was responsible for completely rebuilding the *château* - hence what you see today dates from the 15th century. It stayed in the de Trécesson family until 1773 when it passed to the Le Preste de Châteaugiron family. During the Terror the moderate republican deputy Defermon was hidden here for more than a year. The *château* was later acquired by an army paymaster, the same Nicolas Bourelle de Sivry who is buried in the chapel at St-Jean. In the 19th century it was used for a time by the Morbihan agricultural school and it is now the home of the Comte de Prunelaie.

In the mid 18th century the *château* grounds were the scene of a mysterious and tragic event when an apparent bride-to-be was brought here under duress and buried alive at the foot of a tree. A poacher had taken refuge in the tree at the approach of the 'burial' party and was a witness to the crime. When the party had disappeared into the night, and after some prevarication because of his own precarious position vis-a-vis the law, the poacher and his wife alerted M. de Trécesson, who roused his household and had the unfortunate young woman uncovered, but too late.

Follow the road past the *château*, up to the junction with the D312. Here turn right.

4. After 600m in Le Lidrio, turn left past the no-through-road sign. Bear left through the village and, at the end of the road, continue on the track, following it round to the right and uphill. After a while the track goes straight uphill over bare rock.

5. Towards the top of the bare rock, turn left on another straight track, climbing more gently. Where the track levels off, go right at a T-junction of tracks. Follow this straight track up to a junction of tracks.

Diversion: to see the *Tombeau du Géant* (the Giant's Tomb) go straight on, bearing right. The tomb, a neolithic burial, is to the right of the track after 300m. Return to the junction of tracks to continue the walk.

At the junction of tracks, bear left on the main track to reach a broad T-junction of tracks with a cross, La Croix Lucas, in the centre. Here turn right to return to the car-park 500m away.

Chapel of St-Jean

OTHER WALKS in the area:

Beignon (8½kms ESE) *Boucle de la Vallée de l'Aff* 14kms 4½ hrs
Start from the centre of Beignon.

Campénéac (4kms SW) *Circuit des Eventaillles* 11kms 2¾hrs
Starts from the centre of Campénéac and passes a remarkable old chestnut tree.

Circuit des Landes Rennaises 12kms 3hrs Starts from the centre of Campénéac and takes in a circuit to the north of the town.

PLACES OF INTEREST nearby:

nr. **Concoret** (12kms NW) *Château de Comper - le Centre de l'Imaginaire Arthurien* There is a summer programme of events and displays on the theme of the Arthurian legends.
www.centre-arthurien-broceliande.com

WALK 27: Trégranteur

Length 11kms	Time 2½hrs	Level 2

Location & parking: Trégranteur, 6km south of Josselin, park in car-park behind the church.

Refreshments: none on route.

Trégranteur is one of those place that time has forgotten. Many of the village houses don't seem to have changed at all since they were built several hundred years ago, the church still retains a *colonne de justice*, symbol of the local lord's authority, and the (private) 18th century château behind its impressive wrought-iron gates is only the latest form of a residence that has been in the same family's possession for over 700 years. The walk sets out to find some of the mills that used to 'hum' in the valley of the Sedon and returns via Coët Bugat with its re-built church that still retains a few earlier treasures.

DIRECTIONS

1. **From the car-park walk back to the church and turn right down the street.**

Note the column of justice by the church gate. Quite rare in Brittany, the column is a symbol of the local lord's judicial authority.

Follow the road out of Trégranteur, passing the gate of the *château* on the left, up to the crossroads at La Métairie and turn left.

La métairie - a farm leased on the principle of sharing the profits and losses with the landowner. Often these farms appear larger and more modern, in their time, than other farms, indicating a significant investment by the landowner and a willingness to embrace, or perhaps insist upon, up-to-date farming methods.

In Guilleron, take the first turning on the right and continue on the track, down into the wooded valley and up the other side, ignoring

a track entering from the right.

2. At a Y-junction, turn left downhill on a broad track. Where it meets another track at the bottom, turn right and follow it up to Coët Digo. Here, where a road arrives from the right, take the track to the left. After 50m take the grassy track on the right. Follow this down to bear right on another track along the valley. At the road, bear left along it, and over the river Sedon.

The mill on the left here is the *Moulin de Coët Digo*; note the old mill wheel to the right of the entrance. The Sedon valley was renowned for the number of its mills – none of which is now functioning.

Continue up the road to the trees and fork left. Half way up this straight hill, take the track on the left. After 450m, where the track divides, bear left. At the *Moulin de Roxa* (Rocsa) the track becomes a tarmac road. Continue to a Y-junction. Here bear left and follow the road down to the river, crossing it at the *Moulin de Panros*.

3. Just above the mill buildings, turn sharp right onto a track. This follows the side of the valley, round to the left. Ignore a track on the right descending to a lake. At a tarmac road on the left, bear right to continue on the track.

As the track climbs, the deep roof of the *Manoir de Mongrenier* appears over the skyline to your left. This *manoir* was owned by the family of Guillaume de Montauban, who took part in the famous Battle of the Thirty in 1351. The *manoir* is now English-owned and has

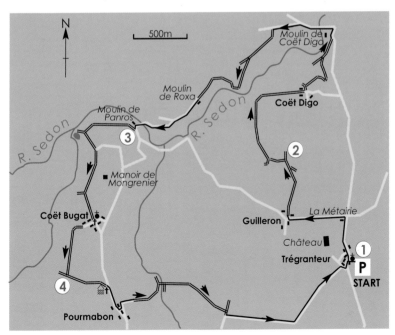

been restored and converted to *gîtes* and *chambres d'hôte* (www.manoir-de-mongrenier.com).

Ignore a track on the right and continue ahead to Coët Bugat.

The initial view of the church is spoilt by a public toilet, but carry on and see the old carved tympanum (17th cent.) set in the churchyard wall.

Turn right by the cross. At the end of the tarmac, continue on the track.

4. After 500m, at a T-junction, turn left. Passing a *fontaine* and *lavoir* on the right, bear right at the road. In Pourmabon take the first road on the left, between houses, then left again. Continue ahead on the grassy track. At the bottom, turn right onto another grassy track crossing the stream. Continue ahead up the hill, ignoring another track from the right. At the T-junction turn right, then left again immediately onto the road. Follow this road for 1.2km back to Trégranteur. Here bear right, then turn left onto the main road to regain the church and the car-park.

Take a look at the old houses in Trégranteur.

OTHER WALKS in the area:

Rouvray (on the Nantes-Brest Canal, 3kms W of Josselin) *Circuit de Pomeleuc* 14kms 3½ hrs Starts at the lock (*écluse*) at Rouvray and follows the canal west to Pomeleuc, returning via Lantillac and the old railway track.

Guéhenno (10kms W) *Sentier des Moulin au Manoir* 11½kms 2¾hrs Start from the market place in Guéhenno, discover more mills on the river Sedon, as well as the fabulous *calvaire* in Guéhenno itself.

PLACES OF INTEREST nearby:

Josselin *Petite Cité de Caractère* (8kms N) *Chateau* and *Doll Museum* 02 .97 22 36 45 Open Apr/May weekends, public and school holidays 2.00-6.00; June-Sept every day 2.00-6.00; mid Jul to end Aug every day 10.00-6.00.

English bookshop opposite the castle gate.

Lizio *Petite Cité de Caractère* (5kms S) see Walk No.3.

WALK 28: Erdeven - La Roche Sèche

Length 12½kms	Time 3½hrs	Level 2

Location & parking: Erdeven, 12kms west of Auray, on the D781 between Belz and Plouharnel. Park in the *Place de la Mairie*.

Refreshments: in Erdeven, none on route.

From the little town of Erdeven with shops and restaurants, this walk meanders through a sort of hotch-potch of holiday homes and farmland to the beach near *La Roche Sèche*. It continues along the beautifully sandy *Plage de Kerminihy* to the mouth of the river Etel, where the *barre d'Etel* sandbank interrupts the surface, threatening shipwreck for the unwary. The return walk is by a different, slightly more rural route. As with many coastal areas, there is some on-going new development here. For this reason the directions make a greater than usual use of distances, rather than identifying features that might change or disappear with time.

DIRECTIONS

1. **From the *Place de la Mairie* walk to the other side of the church and take the *Rue de l'Océan* opposite. At the end in 250m by the STOP sign, bear left to the main road and follow it right for 100m, there turning right into a housing estate.**

At the T-junction in 150m turn left. Follow this road for 700m as it becomes a track, round to the left and through to a T-junction with a road. Here turn right. This road turns left after 100m, then right, then where it bends left again, go ahead onto a track.

2. **After 150m take the track on the left. At the road, turn left, then in 50m right onto a pathway between banks. After 500m cross over another track, then 75m later go left at the fork. Follow this track for 400m over the gorse-covered hill then at the T-junction of tracks go right.**

Soon there is a mobile home park on the right and a marshy area on the left known as the *Etang de Poulbé*. A small menhir stands to the left of the path.

From the main entrance to the mobile home park, continue ahead on the *Chemin des Oyats* for 400m to the T-junction.

3. Here turn left, going past the overhead height gauge, and take the road on the right from the roundabout. Take the first track on the left, through a car-park, and ahead to the shore.

The island ahead is the *Île de Roëlan*. *La Roche Sèche* (the dry rock) is to the right, extending out from the shore - even at high tide it is not entirely submerged.

Turn right along the coast, either along the beach or the fenced path across the dunes.

The path is fenced to protect fragile vegetation - essential for the stability of the dunes.

Passing the extensive car-park behind *La Roche Sèche*, note that the entrances to the beach are numbered. Follow the path behind the beach until you reach entrance number 1.

La Plage de Kerminihy, extends from *La Roche Sèche* to the harbour mouth at Etel. Swimming is possible, though not supervised, and naturism is allowed. Some areas of the dunes behind the beach are protected as a nature reserve, so keep to the paths provided.

4. At entrance No.1, the path turns inland and approaches a car-

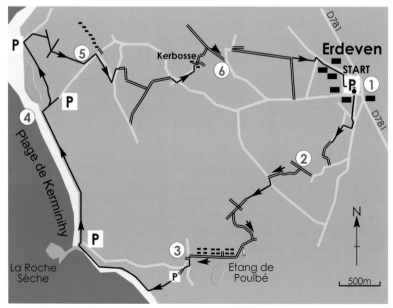

park, but before reaching it, take the path on the left to skirt round behind a marshy area. Follow this path through to a car-park and road near the harbour mouth.

A little way out from the shore at this point one can see waves breaking on the Barre d'Etel, a constantly shifting sandbank at the entrance to the *ria*. Many ships have been wrecked here.

From the car-park go up the road. Just before the brow of the hill, halfway along a grassy lay-by/parking area on the right, a faint path steps over the little bank and climbs the dune ahead. From the top of the dune the ground is level.

Make for the nearby post (an iron girder set into the ground). Then follow the path that heads towards the right hand end of the line of houses in the distance. At a cross path shortly, turn right. At another cross path go straight on towards the road that comes up from the beach.

5. At the road go left and up to the junction, before the overhead barrier. Here turn right. After 300m turn sharp left onto a minor road, then in 100m, right onto a track.

At a T-junction of tracks, turn left. At the road, turn right, then left at the crossroads. This road bends left through the village of Kerbosse and becomes a track. Bearing left at the fork, follow the track through to a T-junction with another track. Here turn right.

6. At the road go left and follow it round to the right. Where the road turns left again, continue ahead on a track (there are two tracks visible here - take the first one). Follow this track for 700m and where it turns right, take the path ahead.

At the road turn left, and then right at the T-junction. Follow the road for 450m to the one-way system and 'no-entry' sign, turning right here to regain the mairie and the starting point.

OTHER WALKS in the area:

Belz (4.5kms NW) *Circuit des Mégaliths* 12km 4hrs Start from car-park *Rue du Général De Gaulle*. Explores much of the coastline of the Ria d'Etel from Kerhuen to the *Moulin de Bignac*.

PLACES OF INTEREST nearby:

Port Louis (20kms W via D781) *Musée de la Compagnie des Indes* Museum of the French East India Company and its trade housed in the old citadel at Port Louis. Open mid-March to Apr 30 1.30-6 every day except Tuesday; 2 May to 31 Aug 10-6.30 every day; 1 Sept to mid Dec 1.30-6 every day except Tuesday. Closed mid Dec to mid March. 02 97 82 56 72 museeindes@mairie-lorient.fr www.lorient.fr/musee.html

WALK 29: Lanvaudan

Length 12½kms	Time 3½hrs	Level 2

Location & parking: Lanvaudan, 6kms east of Plouay. From the centre follow the D145 direction Inzinzac Lochrist for 500m. Park at the old presbytery and tennis courts on the right.

Refreshments: none on route.

Before starting the walk it's worth stopping in Lanvaudan to admire the old stone houses grouped around the church. The walk follows the line of an old railway for much of its route, passing near a Roman bridge hidden in the undergrowth, as well as a calvaire and a chapel, but its real merit lies in the peace of the countryside.

DIRECTIONS

1. From the car-park, cross over the D145 and go up the lane beside the _Ecole St-Joseph_. At the top turn left across the open area used as an agricultural machinery park and cross the road to a footpath entering the woods. Follow this through to another road and turn right. At the junction turn right, then take the lesser road immediately on the left. After 250m at the town exit sign turn right onto a footpath.

Immediately on the left is the _lavoir_ of Fétan-Vorlen.

Continue on this path for 2km.

The path follows the line of the old railway that ran from Plouay to Baud and on to Ploërmel via Locminé. Constructed in 1902 by _Chemins de Fer du Morbihan_, it was one of the first lines in their network of narrow gauge railways. They had all closed by 1947.

After about 1km there is a puddle in the middle of the trackbed and, on the other side of the bank on the left, the _Fontaine du chemin de fer_. This is a naturally occurring spring but also, according to local legend, a point at which engine drivers would replenish their locomotives.

2. Where the track runs along an embankment with a drop on either side, the stream on the left passes under the embankment and re-appears on the right. A few metres further on it flows under a small

stone bridge, said to be Roman. To reach the bridge, descend the track on the right.

Having inspected the bridge, regain the trackbed and 20m further on take the path on the left. Follow this uphill to Rosmenic, emerging on the road and turning right. Note the stone cross behind the hedge on the other side of the road.

The calvaire of Rosmenic, dating from 1695, was erected to protect the villagers from the plague. Its shaft carries the bulbous protrusions, bubons, that symbolise bubonic plague, though these are not as pronounced as on some other *calvaires*.

Walk through the village and, past the last house on the left, just as the road begins to descend, bear left onto a footpath. At the road, go down the road ahead, to the left of the cottage. Follow the road all the way to, then down through the village of Lomelec.

3. About 20m short of the D23, a track leaves on the right. Follow this long, straight track (the old railway again). After 800m it emerges into open country with a stream away to the left in the valley and a field rising on the right. At the end of the field, ignore the sign to the right to Quistinic (GR341) but continue on the line of the old railway. The path, now bordered by a fence on either side, goes through a wood, and crosses a small field with an oak tree in the middle.

At the track go straight on, still following the level path of the the old railway, and straight on over another track. Continue ahead to point (2.) and retrace the route back to Lanvaudan.

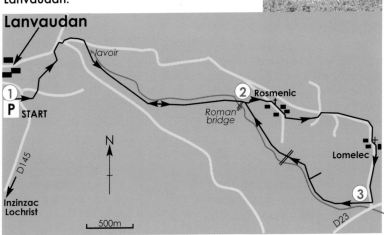

WALK 30: La Chapelle Neuve

Length 12kms	Time 3hrs	Level 2

Location & parking: La Chapelle Neuve on the D117 Baud to Locminé. Park behind the mairie.

Refreshments: none on route.

La Chapelle Neuve, as the name suggests, does have a massive chapel. This walk starts there, and explores the gentle farmland to the south of the village, rising to the beautiful *Forêt Domaniale de Floranges*. This leafy wilderness hides the *Dolmen de Roh Du*, a simple burial chamber of the Late Neolithic/Early Bronze Age. The return journey affords some pleasant views of the heart of rural Morbihan.

DIRECTIONS

1. Take the pedestrian exit from the bottom of the car-park and turn right on the little road. At the T-junction turn left. In La Gare, don't cross the river but fork right on the former railway, past the *Moulin de Kerjosse*.

This is the Baud to Locminé section of the same railway as in Walk no.29 Lanvaudan (see page 94).

Follow the road to a farm on the right, then continue on the footpath, still on the former railway. Cross the river and continue as far as the wood. Here turn sharp left on a track, which climbs through the wood to continue on the other side with fields to the right. Follow the track round to the right and down to the road.

Bear right on the road. After 200m take the track on the right.

2. Where the track begins to descend, go up the track on the left. At the road in Locmaria, turn left, then right immediately. Opposite the chapel on the right, turn left, then right at the T-junction in 50m.

After 100m go straight ahead on a track, signed to Guernic and Petit Guernic. Follow the track right, then 40m past the house on the left, take the track on the left. Enter the wood and, 20m after the fenced enclosure on the left, follow the path to the left. Continue ahead through a gap in the bank and along the right hand edge of a field. Through another gap in a bank, turn right immediately then right again to follow the bank. Pass to the right of another fenced enclosure, then bear right up to a track. Here turn left.

3. After 100m take the footpath to the left. Follow the trodden path through the beech wood, eventually turning northwards and meeting an ancient track. Follow this to the right for 200m, then turn right on a footpath that crosses the track.

At the road, turn right. After 400m turn left, then in 150m left again on a track.

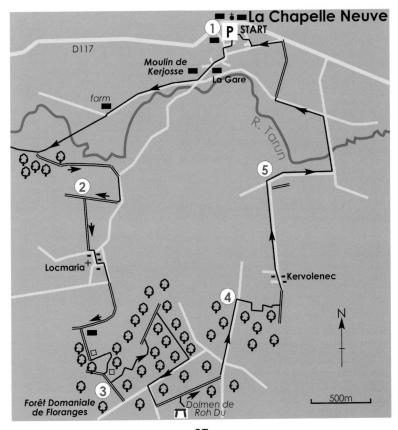

After a further 200m, turn right on a footpath to find the *Dolmen de Roh Du* in about 100m.

There is a multilingual explanatory notice beside the dolmen.

Return to the track and continue right. At the road, turn left and continue ahead at the crossroads.

4. 500m later take the footpath on the right (by a metal sign facing on-coming traffic '*Forêt Domaniale de Floranges*'). Turn right at the bank, then left, left again, then right again. Then left at another bank and downhill, inside the edge of the wood.

At the track, go left, down to the village of Kervolanec, where the track becomes a road. Continue ahead through the village and ahead at the junction, signed *Lan Er Velin*.

5. On the other side of the valley, turn right at the T-Junction (ignoring the track arriving from the right a few metres earlier). At the T-junction at the bottom of the hill, turn left, cross the river Tarun, then turn left at the crossroads (back on the line of the former railway). Opposite metal gates, turn right on a track. Where the track meets the road, turn sharp left on the minor road, signed *Complexe Sportif*.

At a housing estate on the right, turn right up the estate road and take the second road on the left, at the end of which a footpath leads through to the car-park behind the mairie.

OTHER WALKS in the area:

Camors (7km W): *Circuit de l'eau en forêt de Camors* - 11km 3hrs start from Le Petit Bois car-park, blue waymarking. Details from the mairie 02 97 39 22 06 or from Pays d'accueil touristique de la Vallée du Blavet, ZI de Kermarrec, BP 43, 56150 Baud 02 97 51 09 37.

PLACES OF INTEREST nearby:

Baud (7km W.) *Cartopole* Museum of picture postcards. www.cartolis.org Open every day mid June to mid Sept. More limited opening at other times, closed January.

WALK 31: Augan

Length 13kms	Time 3hrs	Level 2

Location & parking: Augan, on the D772 Ploërmel to Guer. Park in the *Place de La Poste*.

Refreshments: in Augan, none on route.

Chapel of St-Nicolas, Le Binio.

The countryside to the south of Augan is beautiful, with rolling hills of well-wooded farmland. The villages, especially Le Binio, are populated and well cared for, with plenty of architectural interest for the practised eye.

DIRECTIONS

1. From the Post Office walk up to the left of the church and take the road to Montneuf, passing the *mairie* on the right and going left at the war memorial. Follow the road out of Augan for 1km. At the bottom of the hill turn left onto the long, straight track and follow it for 2½kms.

This is the old standard gauge railway from Ploërmel to Guer, which was closed in 1960. The river on the right is the Oyon, a tributary of the Aff, which flows into the Oust north of Redon.

2. Just after the track swings left for the second time, take the footpath on the right signed '*Moulin à Eau de Cul Blanc*'. Passing through the gate (this is private land, so please keep to the path), follow the path to the left, down through the woods, crossing the river and turning right with the track on the other side.

The *Moulin de Cul Blanc* is on the right after 100m.

The name *Moulin de Cul Blanc*, literally the White Bottom Mill, according to local tradition, refers to a former miller's habit of sitting on a sack of flour, as a consequence of which he always had a white bottom. (Its more 'correct' name is *le Moulin de Binio*). The mill here, which has an under-shot wheel, was working up until 1940 and is the object of an ongoing restoration project.

From the mill continue up the track, round an S-bend to come out through more gates and continue on the track ahead between fields. At the road turn right, then first left, then left again at the fork 150m later. Follow this road into the village of Le Binio. Uphill, take the second road on the right. The chapel of St-Nicolas is on the left after 100m.

The present Chapel of St-Nicolas at Le Binio dates from the 15th century but is thought to have been founded on a former pagan site by St Winoch c.850 and rebuilt in the 1400s by Guillaume de Montauban, who is buried in the chapel. The cross is 18th century.

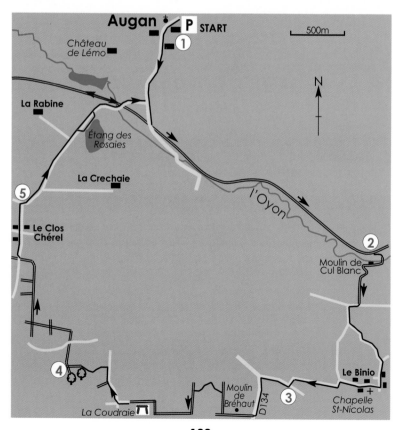

Continue along the village street from the chapel, taking the first road on the left. Follow this round to the right and along to the T-junction.

3. Here turn right. At the next T-junction, turn left on the D134. After 400m take the track on the right. The fence on the right encloses the grounds of the *Moulin de Bréhaut*, a former windmill. At the far corner of the fence, turn right.

Continue for 200m then turn sharp left on a footpath through the trees. Follow the path over rocks and down to a track. Here turn left. Follow the track round to the right, then right again after 300m, then left and in 50m look for a path on the left signed to '*allée couverte*'.

The gallery grave of La Coudraie is a neolithic burial chamber, c.2000BC, constructed in the local stone, purple schist. It appears to have been excavated, probably in the 19th century.

Return to the track and continue. Where the track meets a road, continue ahead, then where it meets a larger road at a crossroads, turn right downhill. Ignore a track on the left where the road bends, continue downhill to take the next track on the left, narrowing immediately to a footpath. Continue into and through a wood and, where the path comes out onto a grassy track, follow that to the left.

4. At a T-junction of tracks turn right, cross over the road and continue on the track, following it left after 100m. At a crossroads of tracks go straight on, then at the next crossroads, go right. Ignoring two tracks on the left, continue on the track around a left hand bend, then turn right along the road.

Walk through the village of Le Clos Chérel, going straight on at the crossroads.

5. At the T-junction, turn right to Augan. Continue to the lake (*L'Étang des Rosaies*) on the right.

Alternative: it is possible to leave the road for 200m, walk alongside the lake, and rejoin the road through the far corner of the picnic area.

Continue on the road, crossing the former railway line.

Alternative: go left along the railway line for a few hundred metres to see the Château de Lémo on the right with its lake in the foreground.

Continue up the *Rue de l'Oyon* and turn left at the T-junction to return to Augan centre and your starting point.

PLACES OF INTEREST nearby:

Monteneuf (10kms SE) *Les Pierres Droites*: an impressive alignment of tall purple schist megaliths, adjacent to a Roman road. There are many other neolithic monuments nearby. (See Walk No.35.)

WALK 32: Bignan

Length 14kms	Time 4hrs	Level 3

Location & parking: Bignan, 4½kms southeast of Locminé on the D1. Park behind the *mairie*.

Refreshments: in Bignan, none on route.

This is a good long ramble. A bit up-and-down as the countryside is typical of central Brittany, with woods, valleys and *chemins creux*. There are some attractive villages, notably Poublay and Guérignan, and the *Fontaine Ste-Nolwenn*, about half way round, makes a pleasant spot for a break.

DIRECTIONS

1. Facing away from the church, take the road to the left of the mairie, signed Locminé. Fork left at the calvaire, signed Colpo. Then fork right uphill, signed '*Garage Kergoat*'. Walk to the left of the garage and continue ahead on a track through the trees. Where the track divides, bear left. Descending to the road, turn left for a few paces then right onto the main road. Bear right at the fork, then take the second road on the right signed La Motte and Cosquer.

(Note the *Calvaire de Treuliec* on the right just before this turning.)

After 200m the road bears left and becomes a stony track. Follow this downhill until a lake becomes visible to the right, then turn left onto another track. Just past a tin shed on the right, take the track on the right.

2. Just before the end of this *chemin creux*, go through a gap in the bank on the left and follow the path round to the right, uphill to the left, then right along the top of a garden. Turn left at the bottom, still within the wood, then uphill to emerge into a field at the corner of the wood. Cross the field by the shortest route to enter the wood on the other side. 50m on, the path meets a road.

Turn left up the road. At the T-junction at the top of the hill, turn right and continue ahead on the sandy track past a house.

3. Ignore the track on the left, continue to just before the end of the track then take the footpath on the right into the wood. Still within the wood but following its edge, bear left round the corner of the field. Bear left across a wide grassy path, then left downhill to meet another wide similar path.

Here turn right. The path descends steeply, turning left and right again around a garden, to reach a road. Turn right on the road and follow it for 600m, through Les Fondrenn.

4. Then turn very sharp left onto a track that goes back towards Les Fondrenn but at a lower level. The track soon becomes a path, which emerges into an open service area. Continue on the track ahead, which later becomes a road.

At the crossroads turn right. 300m past Kerdaniel on the right, take the road sharp left uphill, signed *Fontaine Ste-Nolwenn*. Ignore the track going uphill ahead but follow the road round to the right: soon it becomes a track, arriving after 450m at the *fontaine*.

According to legend, Sainte-Nolwenn was a 6th century virgin and martyr, who was decapitated near Bignan on the orders of a lord whom she had refused to marry. Her feast day is 6th July and she is invoked for curing migraines.

On the opposite side of the track from the *fontaine* are the remains of a *lavoir*.

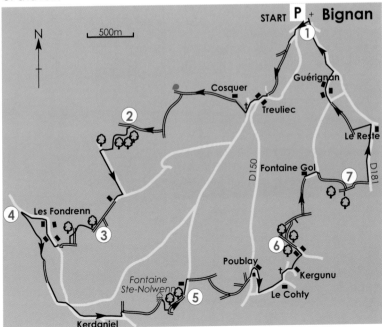

Take the track on the right that passes above the *lavoir*. Follow it down through the woods along the edge of a field, left at the bottom, and climb again to reach a stony track. Here turn left uphill.

5. The track becomes a road, passing a house on the left. 50m later, turn right towards the *Motocross* ground. (Motocross authorised for the 3rd weekend in the month, 2.00 - 5.00pm.)

After 200m take the track sharp right downhill. Ignore tracks to right and left, but at a fork bear right downhill to reach the road. Here bear left, then immediately fork right down into the village of Poublay. Follow the track down between the old houses, then the road round to the right, continuing ahead to the T-junction. Here turn left to Le Cohty.

At the T-junction in Le Cohty, turn left for Kergunu. Pass the calvaire on the left, bear right at the fork and turn left onto a path at the near end of the first house on the left. This narrow, steep path between banks emerges onto a road by some houses. Turn left up the road, continuing ahead where it becomes a track.

6. After 200m, at a fork, bear right. Where a track arrives from the left, bear right along it. Near the top of the hill ignore a bridleway on the right, but continue downhill to go left with the track (ignoring the track ahead). The track continues ahead between fields for 250m, then bends right into a hamlet (Fontaine Gol), becoming a road.

At the bottom of the hill where the road goes left, go right on a track. Ignoring any paths to the left, follow the track to the top of the hill.

7. There, at a T-junction of tracks, go left on the track downhill. At the D181, go left and up to *Le Reste*. At the top of the hill, where a road arrives from the right, take the *chemin creux* on the left. At a T-junction with a track, turn right. At the road, go straight on through the village of Guérignan, continuing ahead to the D181. Turn left here and follow the road into the centre of Bignan.

PLACES OF INTEREST nearby:

Bignan *Château de Kerguéhennec*, contemporary art centre. 02 97 60 44 44 www.art-kerguehennec.com

Réguiny (14kms N) *"Les Sanglots Longs"* Museum of wartime memorabilia with an emphasis on radio.

WALK 33: Malestroit

Length 15kms	Time 3½hrs	Level 2

Location & parking: Malestroit, *écluse* (lock) No.25 on the Nantes-Brest Canal. From the town centre, find the D10 to Sérent but where that turns left out of the market place, go straight ahead (signed *P l'Ecluse* and *Maison de l'eau et de la pêche*). Before the hump-back bridge, turn right and park.

Refreshments: in Malestroit, none on route.

The Nantes to Brest Canal follows the River Oust, with some divergences, from just outside Redon to beyond Rohan. At Malestroit the canal takes a short-cut to avoid a particularly tortuous section of the river. This walk sets out along the canal before picking up the *Voie Verte* (a former railway re-established as a leisure resource) to cross the canalised river further west. The return route is more aligned with the Oust. Herons are quite at home in this terrain - I saw one fly straight up to a reclining cow and walk around it. The final part of the walk re-enters Malestroit past the ruins of the historic *Chapelle de la Madeleine* and across the *Île de la Saudraie*. From here, a stroll around the ancient streets of Malestroit is perfectly possible before returning to the starting point.

DIRECTIONS

1. **Walk along the tow-path to the left, past the lock house, for 2.5kms, passing the *Ecluse de la Née* (No.26) and continuing to the next lock.**

105

Beyond this lock can be seen the point where the canal rejoins the River Oust.

Here leave the canal. Cross the smaller bridge on the left and bear right down the village street. Take the track on the right after the last old house. Follow this track towards the canal and on for 1.5km. After the track swings left, ignore a track on the right and continue up to a straight tarmac road with wooden barriers.

This is the *Voie Verte* (green way), a former railway line from Mauron to Questembert, but now dedicated to walkers and cyclists.

2. Turn right along the *Voie Verte* for 1km. Shortly after crossing the canal, turn right off the *Voie Verte* (just before another bridge) and descend to the track below, turning right along it.

In La Bagotaie, bear right at the road junction. Walk to the left of a farm, towards the N166, turning right alongside it and down to the canal. Here pass under the N166, and follow the track up the other side for almost 400m, before turning right between fields.

At a crossroads of tracks continue ahead, through a farm. At a T-junction with a road, turn right. At the next T-junction, turn left. Then at the next T-junction turn right and follow this road left at the bottom, ignoring tracks right and ahead.

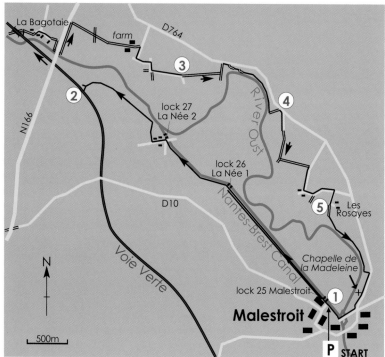

3. After 400m, where the road goes right, continue ahead on a track. At a T-junction of tracks, turn left up to the main road, turn right along it for 50m, then leave by a section of old road on the right. Where this ends, continue ahead to a field, passing down its right hand edge and continuing on a track that descends into the wood. By the river Oust, continue on a footpath. Passing through two sets of wooden posts, turn sharp left and follow the track up to the road.

4. Turn right along the road for 50m then take the road on the right. Continue ahead on a track between fields. Follow it around to the left (ignoring a track ahead). At the T-junction with a little road, turn right. On reaching the houses turn left, then, ignoring a track on the right, continue ahead to take a road on the right signed to *Les Rosayes*.

5. Where the road swings left into *Les Rosayes*, take the track ahead, continuing on the footpath along the river. After almost 1km, the path turns sharp left and comes out on a road on the outskirts of Malestroit. Here turn right and walk down towards the town.

La Chapelle de la Madeleine is where the treaty of Malestroit was signed in 1343, bringing a temporary cessation of hostilities in the 100 Years War between France and England and the Breton War of Succession.

100m after *La Chapelle de la Madeleine* on the right, at a crossroads, turn right down *Rue Notre-Dame*. This leads to a bridge over the river, followed by another bridge over the canal.

Rue Notre Dame passes over the Île de la Saudraie, one of the earliest parts of Malestroit, where an old mill is still working.

At the end of the bridge turn right and follow the canal bank up to the lock and the starting point.

OTHER WALKS in the area

Montertelot (10km N): a 8.5km, 2½ hour circuit begins at the *frayère à brochets* (pike spawning pool) by the Nantes-Brest Canal at Montertelot. Passes wayside crosses, pretty villages and *Les rochers de St Méen*.

St-Laurent (5kms ESE) *Sentier du Houssa*. 12kms 3hrs Start from Place du Four in St-Laurent. Passes the Manoir de Balangeard and the Château de Beaufort overlooking the Oust.

PLACES OF INTEREST nearby:

Malestroit: *Maison de l'eau et de la pêche* - near the lock at the start of the walk - an aquarium, exhibition and museum of local fishing methods.

St-Marcel: (4kms W) Musée de la Résistance Bretonne 02 97 75 16 90 www.resistance-bretonne.com Open all year.

WALK 34: Mohon

Length 15kms	Time 3½hrs	Level 2

Location & parking: Mohon, on the D6 Ploërmel to La Trinité-Porhoët. The entrance to the car-park is opposite the church, in front of the *Maison du Sénéchal*.

Refreshments: in Mohon, none on route.

Mohon is a pleasant small town on the edge of the *Forêt de Lanouée* in the north east corner of Morbihan. Its most interesting building is the *Maison du Sénéchal*, now the town's library, built in 1653 by Julien Gaudin, the notaire of Madame de Sévigné, a society lady whose lively letters have survived. A descendant of his during the Revolution used it as a Chouan recruitment centre. Just outside the town is the *Camp des Rouëts* - the camp of the (Breton) kings. There is an opportunity to visit the site (which also contains a medieval motte) towards the end of the walk. This is a long walk in fairly level country so if you like walking fast, here's a chance to stretch your legs.

DIRECTIONS

1. **Leave the car-park at the far end, turn right at the road and follow it out of Mohon. 500m after the town exit sign take the track on the right. Where a track comes in from the right, go straight ahead up a less used track (gorse and broom either side and down the middle). At the T-junction of tracks, turn sharp left.**

After 800m, at a T-junction, turn right on the road and follow it into Les Courrayes. Here turn left, go past the 'no-through-road' sign and continue on a track when the tarmac ends.

108

2. At a T-junction of tracks, turn left. At the T-junction in Coëtservy turn right and right again onto a track opposite the last house on the left, by an oak tree. Follow this track straight ahead, even where it looks a bit overgrown and unused. Cross the D167 and continue on the road opposite. Where this bends right, bear left and ahead for 1.4km on a long, straight track.

3. At the far end of the wood that has been on the right for 500m or more, turn right at a crossroads of tracks. After 1km, turn left onto the D8 for 50m, then turn right onto another track.

From the brow of the hill you can see the *Forêt de Lanouée* stretching away to the right on the opposite hill.

At a T-junction with a road turn right. At the crest of the rise, turn left by three fir trees onto a track. Follow this down into the valley, going

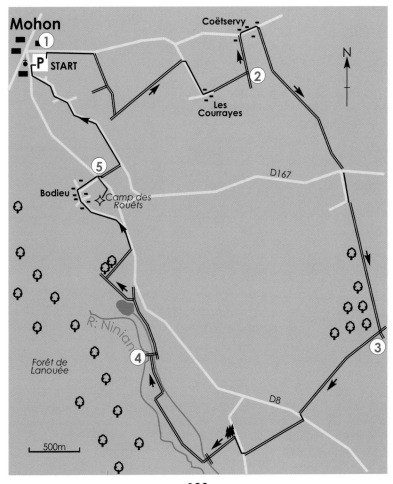

ahead at a crossroads of tracks, over a leet and round to the right.

4. After 1.2km, at a T-junction of tracks, turn right, over the bridge, then sharp left at another T-junction. Follow this track to a lake on the left. At a fork bear left alongside the lake and ahead to the beginning of a wood on the right. Here take the track to the right.

At the road turn left, then take the first road forking left to Bodieu. In Bodieu, go over the crossroads, then take the next on the right and follow it up to the main road.

5. Detour: turn right to visit the Camp des Rouëts, then return to this point.

Go over the main road and down the track opposite.

At the road, turn left. Follow this road up to the T-junction in Mohon and turn right there into the town centre.

Camp des Rouëts

PLACES OF INTEREST nearby:

La Trinité-Porhoët (5.5kms N) Just a quiet town but the beautiful church, dating from the 11th century, has a knave that slopes down to the 13th century west door.

110

WALK 35: Monteneuf

Length 15kms	Time 5hrs	Level 2

Location & parking: Monteneuf, on the D776 from Malestroit to Guer. Park at the *Maison du Randonneur*, behind the church.

Refreshments: in Monteneuf, none on route.

This is a walk of discovery, setting out past three lakes, each one bigger than the last, and visiting dolmens, menhirs and alignments in abundance and, for good measure, a Roman road.
The complete circuit includes an excursion to see the Trembling Rock and back again, taking in an isolated menhir and an alley grave on the way. This section can be omitted if desired, to leave a shorter circuit of 12kms, still packed with interest.

DIRECTIONS

1. Walk to the right of the church back up to the D776 and turn right along it. After 100m turn left onto the grassy area by a lake, taking the path around the left side of the lake and continuing on from the far corner. The path climbs gently through the trees, over some rocks and reaches another lake on the left.

This is the *Etang du Chaperon Rouge* – the lake of the Red Bonnet. A 'red bonnet' revolutionary in the time of Louis XIV is said to have hidden in the rocks here and carved one of them to make a seat.

With the lake on your left, follow the footpath to the end of the lake, going right where it divides. Where it meets a track, turn left.

2. Where the track turns sharp right go straight ahead on a grassy track across open ground. Carry on into the scrub again, and at a crossroads of tracks go ahead to the edge of another lake, the *Etang de Quéhéon*.

Go round the lake either way, but make for the track leaving from the far left corner. After 100m this track comes to a T-junction of tracks.

Here turn left and, just before the track reaches a road, turn right, through a car-park, and continue ahead on another track for 300m. There turn right with the track at a T-junction.

3. After 400m turn right on a path that soon reaches an alley grave (*allée couverte*) called the *Loge Molinais*.

Continue through this site on the footpath, which then twists tortuously through the woods, eventually emerging onto a track.

Here turn left and follow this track for 1.2kms, ignoring any tracks off, whether signed or not, up to a point where the D776 is only 20m away.

Alternative: from here there is the possibility of proceeding directly to Point No.6.

4. Continue ahead on the track, which now diverges from the D776.

After about 400m, just after a large field on the left, a footpath on private land to the left leads to a stone house with a red tiled roof, in front of which, slightly to the left, is a large standing stone, the *Chomet de Couëplan*.

The *Chomet de Couëplan* is one of an alignment, the form of which is hard to see through the undergrowth. When it was mapped in Napoleonic times its height was established as 6m. It is

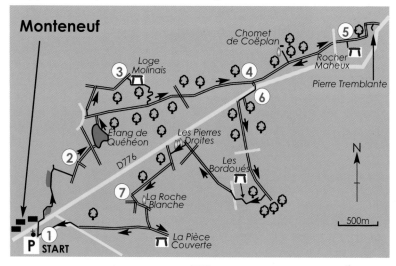

now only 4.5m and the top is lying behind it. The story goes that American soldiers stationed nearby in 1918 lit a fire at the base of the menhir and it was unable to withstand the heat.

Return to the track and continue as before. Eventually the track descends into a valley, crosses a road and continues ahead.

5. At the top of the rise take a footpath on the right leading into the woods to the left of a field (ignoring the track into the field). 100m up this path there are the remains of an alley grave, the Rocher Maheux.

Return to the track and continue as before, following it left downhill, then right at the bottom and round to a point 100m short of the road. Here take the footpath off to the right, which climbs through the woods to reach the *Pierre Tremblante*.

This is a site with many rock outcrops but the *Pierre Tremblante* (the shaking stone) is quite recognisable. According to legend, any girl who succeeds in making the stone move will marry within the year.

Return by the same route all the way back to Point No. 4 and the D776.

6. Turn right along the D776 and take the second track on the left (after about 200m).

Follow this straight track ahead for 500m up to a road, cross over the road and continue ahead. Soon the track continues across farmland and makes for a wood. 100m short of the wood, take the footpath on the right into the trees, indicated by a 'megaliths' finger-post. (Straight on is to the *Voie Romaine* – Roman road – but you will see a Roman road later on this walk.)

The path winds through the trees until it reaches an alley grave, *Les Bordoués*, near the edge of a field on the right.

Continue on from *Les Bordoués*, turning left along the edge of the field and up to the road.

Here turn right along the road. After 100m turn left onto a track. (Notice the old slate fence on the right of this track.)

After 700m go straight on at a crossroads of tracks to reach *Les Pierres Droites*.

Les Pierres Droites is a major alignment of purple schist menhirs. The site also incorporates an interpretation area where there are reconstructions of neolithic dwellings as well as illustrations of how the menhirs might have been moved and then raised. Also nearby is a Roman road, paved with purple schist and with its ditches still visible, running parallel with the D776 100m away.

To leave *Les Pierres Droites*, follow the Roman road away from the track by which you arrived. Leaving the stones, continue ahead on a footpath through the woods, parallel with the main road. After

100m turn left down a track, then after 120m turn right on another track, following this straight ahead for 600m (passing to the right around a metal gated enclosure).

7. Follow the track round to the left, then bear left at a junction of tracks 50m later. Very soon the White Rock (*La Roche Blanche*) appears on the left.

After the White Rock follow the track around to the right, ignore a track on the left shortly afterwards, and go left at an oblique T-junction of tracks to find *La Pièce Couverte* (the covered room) 100m away on the right.

Return to the oblique T-junction and continue straight ahead for 700m.

At the road turn right along it and fork left 100m later, following this road all the way back to the *Maison du Randonneur*.

OTHER WALKS in the area:

Monteneuf *Circuit du Chaperon Rouge* 15km 4hrs. Start at the *Maison du Randonneur*. Wide-ranging triangular circuit to the north of Monteneuf, taking in the valley of the river Oyon.

St-Méen (6kms ESE) *Boucle de la Voie Romaine* Start at Chapelle Saint-Méen. The Roman road referred to linked Angers with Carhaix.

Guer (8kms E) *Boucle du Dran* 11kms 3½ hrs Start in Guer, opposite the *Salles des Fêtes*.

Boucle de la Vallée de l'Oyon 16kms 4¾ hrs Start from the car-park at the *Roche Tremblante*, 2kms out from Guer toward Monteneuf.

Réminiac (4kms W): *Boucle de Réminiac - Circuit des Sculptures* 11kms 2½ hrs Start at *Salle Polyvalente* in Réminiac. (Réminiac holds an arts festival each 1st week of June.)

PLACES OF INTEREST nearby:

Carentoir (8km SE) *La Ferme du Monde* Breton village with 400 animals from 5 continents. www.lafermedumonde.com

WALK 36: Poul Fetan & Quistinic

Length 15kms	Time 4hrs	Level 3

Location & parking: Quistinic lies just west of the D3, half way between Bubry and Baud. From Quistinic follow signs to Poul Fetan, where there is a large car-park for visitors to the 17th century village.

Refreshments: at Poul Fetan in season, and Quistinic.

Poul Fetan was a village in ruins until rescued in 1977 and gradually restored from then onwards. Today it is one of Morbihan's principal tourist attractions, aiming to show all aspects of daily life in a rural village of the 17th century. A morning visit and lunch at Poul Fetan, followed by this walk in the afternoon, make a very pleasant day out, into which the 21st century need hardly intrude at all.

DIRECTIONS

1. From the Poul Fetan car-park, turn right on the road, walk through the village of Hévédic and continue on the footpath. At a junction of paths, continue ahead. At the next junction bear right on a grassy track downhill. Continue ahead for several hundred metres, then follow the track across a field to a wood on the other side. Where a larger track arrives from the left, bear right along it. When this track curves left and heads towards the farm (Kervéhennec), go right onto another smaller track.

2. At the little house, turn right and go down the *chemin creux*. At a T-junction of paths, turn right, downhill to Kermoizan, here joining a little tarmac road. Where the road goes right, go to the left of the house, bearing right at a fork shortly afterwards. Then bear left to emerge on the road near a T-junction.

Take the road signed 'Inzinzac-Lochrist' and 'Hennebont'. After 100m, fork right onto a path. Follow this through to Locunolé. Here, go to the right of the first building and head for the chapel.

The name Locunolé (Lok-Gwenole in Breton) indicates a place where the 5th century St-Gwénolé is venerated. It was he who founded the famous abbey at Landévennec in Finistère. The chapel at Locunolé dates from 1696.

Take the road to the right of the chapel.

3. At the T-junction turn right, then right again immediately, down a *chemin creux*. Where it divides, bear left ahead, then bear right onto a track. At a T-junction of tracks, bear left, then left again at the road.

After 200m take the track into the woods on the right, bearing left where it divides in 50m. Where it divides again, bear right uphill to Rosnen.

4. Go to the right of the house and turn left onto the little road. At the junction bear right. Follow the road through Kermèze and Kerhoué, then turn left by the cross.

5. At the junction in La Villeneuve Jamain, turn right onto a footpath. Where the path bends left, go ahead onto another path. Where the path meets a track, bear right along it.

At the road, continue ahead along the road. After 200m, take the little road on the right, continuing ahead on a grassy track, along the right hand edge of a field, down into the valley, across a little stream and straight on up the other side.

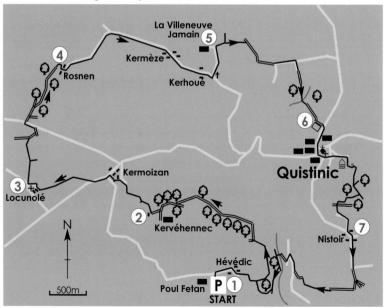

6. Emerging by the cemetery wall, bear left along it and turn right at the road to walk up into Quistinic. Continue past the church, then round to the left by the war memorial, following signs to *Fontaine St-Mathurin* to find the *fontaine* and *lavoir* in a valley.

Go down to the left of the *fontaine*, then follow the grassy path around to the left. Crossing the head of a valley, continue bearing left, up to the right of a water source. Turn right through a gap in the bank, then along the path to the right. Ignore a path arriving from the left and a little path ahead shortly afterwards at a right-hand bend.

Where a track crosses the path, continue ahead downhill. At the bottom, continue ahead on the road, up to Nistoir.

7. Here bear left on the road, bearing right at the junction shortly afterwards. At a left bend 300m later, go ahead on the track. Where it divides in three, go right. Go round to the right at the top of the hill, then ahead on the grassy track. Continue ahead along the top of a field on the left. At the far corner of the field, go down the track to the left.

At the road bear right, then take the first road on the left. After 50m take the track sharp right. Cross the stream and turn left at the T-junction of paths. Where the path divides, bear right uphill. Where the path divides again, bear right. At the T-junction of paths at the top of the hill, turn left to retrace your outward route to Poul Fetan.

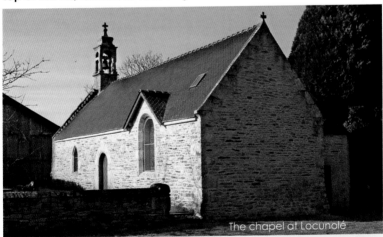
The chapel at Locunolé

PLACES OF INTEREST nearby:

Poul Fetan: *village breton d'autrefois* - open Apr/May 2.00-6.30. Jun-Sept 2.00-6.30, with guided visits 11.15 to 12.30.
July/Aug 1.00-7.00, with guided visits 10.45-1.00. Closed Sept 25th to March 31st. 02 97 39 51 74 www.poul-fetan.com

PLACES OF INTEREST in MORBIHAN

A selection of tourist attractions and places of interest, listed alphabetically by their location, with a reference to the nearest walk in this book, where further details are noted.

Arzon (Walk 16): *The 17th century tide mill at Pen Castel*

The *Butte de Caesar* (tumulus)

Baud (Walk 30): *Cartopole* Museum of picture postcards

Béganne (Walk 13): *Château de Léhélec*

Bignan (Walk 32): *Château de Kerguéhennec,* contemporary art centre

Carentoir (Walk 35): *La Ferme du Monde* Breton village with 400 animals from 5 continents

Baud

Carnac (Walks 12 & 14): *Neolithic Alignments of menhirs*

Musée de Préhistoire

Archaeoscope

The Tumulus of Kercado

Elven (Walk 18): *Château de Largoët*

Gueltas (Walk 2): Maison de l'Environnement

Hennebont (Walk 1): Haras National

Bottle monster at the 'Maison de l'Environnement', Gueltas

Josselin

Josselin (Walks 3 & 27): *Petite Cité de Caractère*

> *Château*
>
> *Doll Museum* in château stables
>
> *English bookshop* opposite the castle gate

Langonnet (Walk 20): church dating from the end of the 11th century

La Trinité Langonnet (Walk 20): interesting church and an elaborate fontaine a short walk away

La Trinité-Porhoët (Walk 34): church, dating from the 11th century

Le Faouët (Walks 8 & 20): *17th century market hall*

> *La Chapelle de St-Fiacre*
>
> La Chapelle Ste-Barbe

Le Guerno (Walks 6 & 21): *Parc Animalier et Botanique de Branféré*

Lizio (Walk 3): *Petite Cité de Caractère*

> *L'Univers du Poète Ferrailleur*
>
> *Musée des Vieux Métiers*
>
> *Insectarium*

Poète Ferrailleur, Lizio

119

Malansac (Walk 6): *Parc de Préhistoire de Bretagne*

Malestroit (Walk 33): *Petite Cité de Caractère*

Maison de l'eau et de la pêche

Melrand (Walk 17): *Village de l'An Mil.* A museum based on a reconstruction of a Breton village in the year 1000AD

Monteneuf (Walks 31& 35): *Les Pierres Droites,* neolithic alignment

Muzillac (Walk 21): *Moulin de Pen Mur.* Old mill making paper using traditional 18th century methods

Malestroit back street

Plouay (Walk 11): *Véloparc* - a space entirely devoted to the bicycle, including a museum

Plouharnel (Walk 12): *Musée de la Chouannerie*

Port du Crouesty (Walk 16): *Cairn du Petit Mont* - a neolithic cairn on promontory at the mouth of the Port du Crouesty

Pont-Scorff (Walk 25): *L'Odysseum*

La Maison du Scorff

La Cour des Métiers d'Art

Zoo de Pont-Scorff

Port Louis (Walks 14, 25 & 28): *Musée de la Compagnie des Indes*

Port Louis from the citadel

Poul Fetan (Walk 36): recreation of life in 17th century Breton village

Réguiny (Walk 32): *"Les Sanglots Longs"* Museum of wartime memorabilia

Rochefort-en-Terre (Walk 6): *Petite Cité de Caractère Château*

Sérent (Walk 3): *Musée de Costumes Bretons*

Ste-Anne d'Auray (Walk 4): elaborate church (major centre of pilgrimage) WW1 war memorial *Historial - Musée de Cire* (waxworks museum)

Ste-Anne d'Auray

St-Aignan (Walk 24): *Musée de l'Electricité*

St-Armel (Walk 22): *Les Marais de Lasné* - working salt marshes

St-Gildas-de-Rhuys (Walk 22): 11th century abbey church of St-Gildas

St-Marcel (Walk 33): *Musée de la Résistance Bretonne*

St-Nicolas-des-Eaux (Walk 17): waterfront with cafés/restaurants *Chapelle de St-Nicolas* - decorated beams dated 1534

St-Pierre-Quiberon (Walk 12): *Cromlech of St-Pierre-Quiberon Alignments of St-Pierre-Quiberon*

Suscinio (Walks 16 & 22): *Château de Suscinio*

Cromlech, St-Pierre-Quiberon

Index of places

Walks in Morbihan

Date   Place

Comments and suggestions:

Please return to: Red Dog Books
                  29410 Plouneour-Menez, France

--- ✄ --

Walks in Morbihan

Date   Place

Comments and suggestions:

Please return to: Red Dog Books
                  29410 Plouneour-Menez, France

Walks in Morbihan

Date   Place
Comments and suggestions:

Please return to: Red Dog Books
                      29410 Plouneour-Menez, France

Walks in Morbihan

Date   Place
Comments and suggestions:

Please return to: Red Dog Books
                      29410 Plouneour-Menez, France

other RED DOG books

Explore Brittany

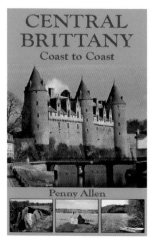

Walking Brittany

by Judy Smith

28 walks covering spectacular coast, hills and forests, varied water courses and traditional countryside. The text includes full directions and provides atmospheric accounts of places of interest on the routes - megalithic monuments, châteaux and sacred structures with their associated legends.

ISBN: 0 9536001 4 9

978 0 9536001 4 4

£9.95,   15€

Central Brittany
Coast to Coast

by Penny Allen

The key to a landscape alive with legend and places of historic significance. Covers a north to south section of Brittany from the pink granite coast to the Gulf of Morbihan. Also included is a selection of detailed scenic walks with full directions and points of interest.

ISBN: 0 9536001 6 5

978 0 9536001 6 8

£8.99,   13€50

www.reddogbooks.com

other RED DOG books

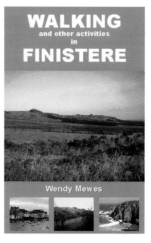

Finistere
**Things to see and do at
The End of the World**

by Wendy Mewes

14 separate tours by car,
with maps, directions and
suggestions for places to visit
and landscape to explore in
the most distinctively varied
department of Brittany.

ISBN: 0 9536001 2 2

978 0 9536001 2 0

£8.99,   13€50

Walking
**and other activities in
Finistere**

by Wendy Mewes

36 circular walks with maps and
directions, and suggestions for
45 more. Also included is key
information for other outdoor
activities - golf, riding, water-
sports, fishing and cycling.

ISBN: 0 9536001 3 0

978 0 9536001 3 7

£8.99,   13€50

www.reddogbooks.com

other RED DOG books

Discover Brittany

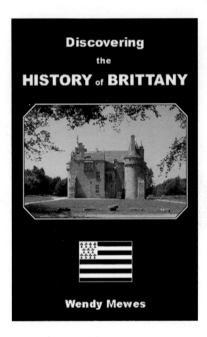

Discovering the History of Brittany

by Wendy Mewes

A concise account of the history of this extraordinary
region. It offers a clear picture of a complex subject
through the presentation of people and places that
have coloured events from pre-historic times to the
present day. Colour photographs and line drawings
illustrate many aspects of Brittany's historical heritage.

ISBN: 0 9536001 5 7   978 0 9536001 5 1

£8.99, 13.50 euros

www.reddogbooks.com